James Slack tells of the magnificent contributions of one of the 80% of units that provided support to Soldiers and Marines in the field. It also tells the often-neglected story of a Soldier's spouse, the true unsung hero.

I highly recommend Dear Janie: Letters Home from the 85th Evacuation Hospital, Vietnam, 1971 to anyone, but especially those who served in Vietnam, their families, and friends. I believe it provides unique insight into what it was like to live and work in a military trauma facility in a combat zone.

You will learn, and feel, much from this personal story of a young couple's life and love in time of war. They are truly gracious to share this family treasure.

— **Michael H. Taylor, Major General, U.S. Army (Retired)**

Dear Janie: Letters Home from 85th Evacuation Hospital, Vietnam, 1971 *is unique in that it describes the last days of the Vietnam War in one of the most remote hospitals in the theater. It is frank and honest about a tough period in American history.*

— **Bill Cameron, Colonel, US Army, Retired**

As I read Dear Janie, *I recalled my experiences as a 21-year-old Army nurse assigned to the 91st Evacuation Hospital in Chu Lai, Vietnam in January 1970. This book is an important read for anyone interested in firsthand accounts of veterans of the Vietnam War.*

— **Elaine Cameron, RN, First Lieutenant, US Army Nurse Corps**

Dear Janie

Letters Home from 85th Evacuation Hospital

Vietnam, 1971

Copyright © 2023 James Slack
Printed in the United States. All rights reserved.

No part of this book may be reproduced in any form or by a electronic or mechanical means, including information storage and retrieval systems, without permission in writing from the publisher, except by a reviewer, who may quote brief passages in a review.

Contact the author: jamesslack65@yahoo.com

Cover Design by Rebecca Byrd Arthur
Interior Design by Danielle H. Acee, authorsassistant.com

Paperback ISBN: 979-83936695-3-9
Hardcover ISBN: 979-83947880-9-3

Cataloging-in-Publication Data
Slack./James
Dear Janie: Letters Home from 85th Evacuation Hospital, Vietnam, 1971
p. cm.

First edition 2023

Acknowledgements

Initially, the purpose of this narrative was to condense my long-lost letters from a war a long time ago in a country far, far away into a simple read that my children, grandchildren, and beyond might find of interest someday. Those efforts surprisingly evolved into this book. However, the underlying intent never changed and this is written to and for my daughters Shannon, Jessica, and Cameron and their children Grant, Rhett, Emma Jane, Clara, Addie, Gideon, and Gabriel.

My best friend, and the love of my life, my wife Janie, truly ensured that our story got written, especially for our family and descendants. Had it not been for a fall and prolonged recovery subsequent to surgery on my rotator cuff, I would never have had the patience to sit still long enough to complete this task. Without Janie's unwavering support, patience, advice, and much better than my technical skills, this work would never have seen the light of day.

My cousin, Edward Bruce, wrote a book about the WWII experiences of his father, Doyle Edward Bruce, in 2022. He strongly encouraged and coached me in the creation of this book. Thank you, Edward.

I also appreciate my Authors' Assistant, Danielle H. Acee, whose patience, encouragement and guidance were truly invaluable.

Cameron, Shannon, Janie, James, Jessica

Foreword

The irony of James Slack's book is almost palpable....

On February 7th 1970, I was a Navy Corpsman assigned to 3rd Force Reconnaissance Company, located at Phu Bai, in northern I Corps of what was then South Vietnam. On the morning of that fateful day, I was taken to the 85th Evac Hospital to remove the bodies of Sergeant Arthur Garcia, Lance Corporal James Fuhrman, and Corporal Ted J. Bishop, from an incoming helicopter. Ted Bishop had been my Team Leader on more than a dozen long range reconnaissance missions in the A Shau Valley, from October of 1969, until February of 1970.

That morning "Team Snaky" had been ambushed by a North Vietnamese Army company resulting in the deaths of the three aforementioned Marines and the wounding of Lance Corporal Paul Keaveney, shot five times while returning fire with his 40mm grenade launcher. Paul would become a patient at the 85th Evacuation Hospital until he was stabilized and then medically evacuated to the Yokosuka Naval Hospital in Japan several days later.

The 85th Evacuation Hospital was located at the northern end of the Phu Bai base and was where all of our casualties were taken for emergency hospitalization for wounds and injuries sustained in combat. It was a Godsend for us to have such a wonderful medical hospital so close to us for obvious reasons, not to mention the psychological boost it provided, knowing that if we were in need of immediate medical care it was there.

Having been hospitalized for two weeks at the 85th Evacuation Hospital in the winter of 1969, after drinking water from a stream poisoned with dead pigs by the NVA, I can attest to the great quality of care given to its patients.

James Slack's book details his entry into the United States Army, his training as a Medical Service Corps officer and his assignment as Registrar to the 85th Evacuation Hospital, at Phu Bai, in the summer of 1971.

This book describes in great detail the daily events which occurred in a hospital, that treated more than 67,000 patients during 1969-1971! The personalities of the hospital's doctors, nurses, medics and patients are brought to life, as are the daily medical triumphs and tragedies within the 85th Evacuation Hospital.

This is the first book that I have read that describes the "inner workings" of a US Army evacuation hospital during the Vietnam War and written by an officer who was there to see and experience all of it.

James uses his letters to his wife, Janie, as the chronological vehicle that moves his readers, almost day-by-day, in his world within a medical unit plagued with drug use, self-inflicted gunshot wounds, racial discord, and the treatment of both American military patients and enemy patients as well. This, combined with his personal joy of receiving letters from home and the weekly letters that describe the growth of his baby daughter, Shannon, complete this man's story.

Here it is, warts and all, of one man's incredible journey in Vietnam from September of 1971 until January of 1972, as the Admissions Officer, and then Registrar of the 85th Evacuation Hospital at Phu Bai.

His story is, in a word, remarkable!

— Major Bruce H. "Doc" Norton, USMC (Ret), author,
Force Recon Diary, 1969, Force Recon Diary, 1970, **and others**

Letters Home from 85th Evacuation Hospital Vietnam, 1971

Janie and James
July 1969, Houston, Texas

James in Vietnam

Preface

In January 2022, my wife Janie stumbled across a shoebox containing all the letters I had written to her from Vietnam. We were ecstatic to find them as we had given them up for lost after fifty-plus years. We did have the letters she wrote me, but they only told a small part of our story. For several evenings, we sat on our couch reading them and found them quite enlightening. I remembered very little of the events described, which surprised us, given the gravity and, at times, the mystery of the situations.

This is an almost daily journal of events I experienced in Vietnam. They are clearly not combat stories, just my stories.

Janie does a lot of genealogy and is often frustrated to discover our relatives who must have experienced at least interesting, and possibly exciting, dangerous, and/or historical events, but left no personal stories or records for posterity. She insisted that our stories must be preserved in a readable form, at least for our immediate family, because they give a firsthand description of not only the declining days of the Vietnam War, but our personal experiences that accompanied them. Of course, she was right. We reflected on the many obituaries and eulogies we've read or heard over the years that left us regretting that we had not known to ask about some interesting part of the deceased's life. The ultimate goal became then, to edit and compile our letters, removing the more personal and mundane entries, and produce a historical narrative that our family and others might find interesting.

Editing out the personal exchanges risks glossing over the reflections of young love that we shared in our written words, and that became a strong but largely un-shareable part of our story. There were no support groups that Janie ever found; almost no friends who were experiencing her loneliness, questions, and concerns for her husband; and certainly, no social media. I unabashedly admit that I fell in love all over again with Janie during this endeavor as I read of her struggles raising our toddler, and saw her unwavering love and devotion to me and our future.

***

The advent of Vietnam television documentaries has meant much to Vietnam vets. While there, what we saw and experienced was largely just a snapshot in time. At the 85th Evacuation Hospital, we seldom knew what was transpiring in the field. We could only judge action by the number or lack thereof of casualties. Years later, the documentaries helped fill in the blanks of what was going on within the political and military command scenes, although they also illuminated various wise and not so wise decisions that affected so many of our lives. Looking back, I don't envy our leaders and the decisions they had to make. It's not easy even now to Monday-morning quarterback. If only mankind could learn from its history!

Lastly, I must add my undying appreciation and admiration for all the men whose very jobs seemed designed to put them at risk. Assuredly, all of us who had less than combat assignments felt in awe of them and never envied the tasks they were given. On behalf of all those who served with the 85th, I offer them our appreciation for the sacrifices they made and endured during a very difficult time in our country. I also offer our regrets and lifetime condolences to the many loved ones of those service members who were killed or physically or mentally crippled, for we saw with first-hand immediacy the injuries they endured and marveled at the courage such fine young men demonstrated. We occasionally received the remains of Soldiers who had been missing and could only imagine the angst and despair their families had endured. May God grant you all peace with each passing day.

An Uncertain Future

I attended the University of Texas at Austin from 1964 to 1968. Just out of Lufkin High School in East Texas, I think I had probably heard of Vietnam but certainly knew nothing about the issues transpiring there. However, I vividly remember becoming more aware as my college career progressed. What is now Austin-Bergstrom International Airport was then Bergstrom Air Force Base, and it was home for many F-4 Phantom fighter jets and B-52 bombers. The roar of military jets became a common sound over Austin as things heated up in Nam. By my senior year, the prospect of serving in the military was assured, as the draft was taking all able-bodied men as soon as they graduated from college. Exceptions were allowed for those accepted to medical, dental, and veterinary schools. I applied to veterinary school at Texas A&M with my pre-med vertebrate zoology degree (along with 800+ others trying for one of the 120 slots) but was not accepted. Hoping that there might be some postgraduate loophole I was unaware of, I also applied for master's degree programs at the University of Wyoming, Texas A&I University, and Stephen F. Austin State University in biological sciences and was accepted by each.

I heard that some draft boards were granting deferrals for teachers in critical curriculum areas. My plan became to teach a year or so, do some graduate work to improve my GPA, and try again for vet school. Therefore, I submitted my name to the Texas State Teachers Association as a science teacher and was stunned to receive offers from twenty-eight high schools within two weeks. There was much demand, especially for male teachers! I accepted Crockett, Texas ISD's offer primarily because their superintendent, Bob Hawes, said he knew the draft board chairman in Lufkin and assured me he could get a deferral for me.

I graduated from UT on a Friday in August 1968 and the following Monday walked into a Crockett High School classroom as the new head of the science department. I had had no teacher training and was granted a Texas emergency teaching certificate due to a critical shortage of high school science teachers. Unfortunately for my students and me, there was no available curriculum, as Crockett was in the process of adopting new textbooks for my subjects. Therefore, evenings in my one-room, fifty-dollar-a-month, garage apartment were consumed in preparing lesson plans for the next day's classes. I taught two chemistry and two biology classes plus a study hall each day. My salary for the year was $4,800, and to supplement that, I was given a bus route to drive each morning and afternoon which earned me another fifteen dollars a week, as I recall. I resigned from that "perk" after two weeks. Three hours out of each day was just too exhausting, although it was eye opening to see the impoverished conditions with which some of my students were struggling. I actually enjoyed my short teaching career once I got into a routine, and I occasionally still hear from a former student. However, it was without a doubt the hardest work for the least pay I ever experienced, before or since. Then, to my surprise, in November, I received notice that I had been drafted by the U.S. Army. However, my induction date was extended to the end of the school year due to the critical science teacher shortage.

I was now a "lame duck," as far as making any future career decisions. Everything was on hold for the six months remaining in the school year, plus the at least two years that the Army had me. The one thing I was sure of was that I did not want to become a "grunt" (Infantry Soldier) in Vietnam. My father, Leslie Irving Slack, had been an infantry squad leader and then a POW in the European theater of WWII. He was captured by the Germans and my mother, Lavigna Foster Slack, didn't know if he was dead or alive for six months. My brother David was born while my father was MIA (missing in action). I hoped to avoid Infantry.

Shortly before my college graduation, I, along with a busload of other soon-to-be graduates, was sent to San Antonio for a preinduction physical examination. I passed with flying colors. That is, I was breathing and had a heartbeat. That induced me to visit the Air Force and Navy recruitment centers in Austin. The USAF was not in need of any recruits. The USN only had openings for wannabe pilots. I called my uncle Albert Slack and asked his thoughts, since he was a Naval ace who flew Hellcats off carriers in the Pacific during WWII. He promptly dissuaded that notion, assuring me that flying jets into combat from an aircraft carrier was the most dangerous job in all the military.

Fortunately, my UT organic chemistry lab partner, Harvey "Skip" Slocum, had served as a combat medic in Vietnam. He was totally empathetic with my quandary and urged me to investigate the Medical Service Corps, a little-known branch of the Army. It required a bachelor's degree, preferably in biological sciences, and offered a direct commission. No ROTC or OCS (Officer Candidate School) required. However, it mandated a three-year commitment. That seemed like a no-brainer to me, but selection for an MSC commission was understandably very competitive. Coincidentally, Skip's father was the commanding officer of the Medical Field Service School at Ft. Sam

Houston in San Antonio where all Army medical specialties were trained. Skip gave me Col. Slocum's number and insisted I call him. We had a very congenial conversation, and Col. Slocum sent me an info packet and arranged for me to be interviewed by a major and a captain who seemed to be tasked with securing new MSC officers. When they asked how I even knew of the Medical Service Corps, I mentioned that Col. Slocum had told me all about it. I remember the two officers glancing at each other, and shortly thereafter, I received notification that I was to report to Ft. Sam Houston in April for my induction into the U.S. Army Medical Service Corps.

***

Jane Blake Ford was from Houston. She and I started dating the spring of our sophomore year at the University of Texas in Austin. We were introduced by Mary Slater, a Zeta Tau Alpha sorority sister of Janie's who was from Lufkin. Now that we were both out of college, we were getting pretty serious. Janie was employed by the Texas Liquor Control Board in Austin and made a couple of forays to Crockett to visit me. These visits generated quite the gossip mill in the high school about the young science teacher and his girlfriend. Things got a little more serious when I received my orders to report to Ft. Sam Houston on May 4, 1969. There, I would undergo eight weeks of training in the Army Medical Department Officer Basic Course. Upon completion, I was to report to the U.S. Army Dental Unit at Ft. Gordon, GA. Although the future picture was becoming somewhat clearer, the probable twelve-month tour in Vietnam still loomed heavily over us. Fortunately, our college romance had had time to mature, and we decided to take a leap into the unknown together. I asked her to marry me while I was in training, and we wanted to establish our new home in Georgia together, so decided on a wedding date of July 18, 1969. I'm not sure Janie's mom Jane Stroud Ford, or her father Kenneth Bowen Ford ever forgave me for giving them only five weeks to plan the wedding of their firstborn daughter. It was a whirlwind, but it turned out perfect, and we have been happily married now for fifty-three years.

I made some great friends in Crockett, including Johnny Dean, Tommy Welch, his brother Bobby Welch, and Bill Brown. They each served as ushers in my wedding. We were all just out of college, except for Bobby, who was a student at Sam Houston State University. We hung out together when they were in town and grabbed many a chicken fried steak at the Royal Cafe. I loved eating at the Royal because its food was really good, but especially because its walls were covered with some of the largest deer racks I had ever seen. Times were good! Hunting and fishing were my passions and still are.

Crockett High School substituted with existing faculty members to finish out the remaining month of my contract, and I was glad to not have to deal with composing and grading final exams. The faculty had a small farewell party for me, and my students had fun making up goofy goodbye cards and poems that I learned to treasure as their way of expressing affection and appreciation. Some probably were hoping for forgiveness for pranks played on me earlier in the year, which later became fond memories...but not so much at the time. For example, putting a live rat in my desk drawer, a six-foot coachwhip snake coiled up in a small box left on top of my desk, shoe polishing messages on the inside of my car windows, and chaining and padlocking my car doors. The experienced teachers assured me pranks were evidence that kids liked me, and that they must have really liked me a lot.

Medical Service Corps Training

The Army's Medical Field Service School has been at the forefront in developing innovative battlefield medical treatments for over 100 years. Its first home was at Carlisle Barracks beginning in 1920, and it was moved to Ft. Sam Houston as part of the Brook Army Medical Center in 1946. All Army medical profession officers start there for their initial indoctrination and training as soldiers. Classes were structured for physicians, dentists, veterinarians, nurses, and Medical Service Corps officers. Early on, we were all taught to march which included drill and ceremony. This proved to be very entertaining at times. Classes were typically composed of about sixty students, and each had its own commanding officer who would appoint a student to lead the drill and ceremony for that day. I remember watching classes, particularly physicians, march through garbage cans or bicycle racks because their leader, or the class members, hadn't learned the commands to turn them. We MSCs took marching and the commands a little more seriously knowing we might be in a position of command someday. Doctors, not so much. Many of them had been drafted and were not happy about it. Some had established practices already, while others were fresh out of school or residencies, so their situational angst was understandable. For others, the government had paid for their education, so they were just repaying their obligation and they were usually the most mellow.

All officers were housed in bachelor officers' quarters, which were in typical barracks buildings, but consisted of individual bedrooms as opposed to the open-dorm settings of junior enlisted soldiers. Meals were served in mess halls, and the food was unmemorable, except for the famous breakfast feast known to all soldiers as SOS or "s--t on a shingle," which was some kind of meat drowned in cream gravy and splatted on a slice of toast. It was everywhere I ever had breakfast in a military mess hall and was actually fairly palatable, all things considered. Most of us had our vehicles with us and could come and go after class but with a curfew each night. My intro to the military went pretty well, except for getting a ticket from an MP for parking on the grass, getting razed by some enlisted soldiers for wearing my garrison cap backward as I crossed the quadrangle, and then getting chewed out by a Lieutenant Colonel for not wearing my headgear on campus. Mine had been stolen, and I was actually on my way to purchase another when he spotted me.

We attended classes each day and were required to pass exams in order to receive our certificates of mandatory training. All MSCs completed the following courses:

- Battle indoctrination
- Chemical, biological, radiological and nuclear training
- Code of conduct
- Emergency medical care
- Geneva Convention
- Military justice
- Survival, escape, and evasion
- Weapons familiarization in arms

Our training in emergency medical care was fairly comprehensive, and I remember that we practiced starting IVs on each other and learned how to give injections, perform tracheostomies, treat sucking chest wounds, control bleeding, and insert catheters.

For field exercises and training, we were bused to Camp Bullis, which was a few miles west of San Antonio. It was very rocky, hilly, and thorny. There we were familiarized with the M14 rifle as well as different types of booby traps in use by the North Vietnamese. We learned firsthand the effects of tear gas and how to properly don gas masks. Night training included light (illumination) discipline and suppression, compass reading, and how to silently set up and break down camp. We also went through a night obstacle course that included crawling beneath barbed wire with machine-gunned tracer bullets zipping overhead while explosions were triggered in the mud nearby. My biggest concern, however, was of stumbling upon a rattlesnake in the dark, which seemed to me a very real possibility considering the terrain in which we were stumbling. Fortunately, I heard of no such reports, and it's probably safe to assume some of my new northern friends were even more relieved than I was.

Graduation for my class #8 from the Army Medical Officer Basic Course (Medical Service Corps) occurred June 27, 1969. To my knowledge, most of us received an MOS (Military Occupation Specialty) of 3506, which was Field Medical Assistant. Our primary function was to take as much administrative work off the medical specialists as possible. I was ordered to report to Ft. Gordon, Georgia, on July 7 as Administrative Assistant to the Post Dental Surgeon. While in Crockett, I had bought a 1968 Dodge Coronet 500 from Wayne Williams Motor Company. It had been owned by Wayne's father-in-law, Dr. John L. Dean. Also, he was my friend Johnny

Dean's dad and had been my mother's ear, nose and throat doctor for years. The car was very spiffy. I had been driving a '63 Impala that I really liked, but the rear windshield leaked badly, and I decided to upgrade rather than repair the Chevy. Upon Basic graduation, I drove my Dodge to Augusta, Georgia, to meet the future. I was received at the post dental surgeon office by a very welcoming group, including Col. Howard McCall, commanding officer; Maj. Leo Eandiorio, executive officer; and First Sergeant Ross Gill; as well as two civilian secretaries. I spent some of the first few days looking for a home for Janie and me and settled on the Williamsburg South Apartments in Augusta, about five miles from the Army post.

The Wedding

Even though I had only been at Ft. Gordon for two weeks, I was granted a week's leave to go back to Houston to get married. I flew back on a Thursday, attended a party that night, a rehearsal dinner Friday night, and got married in the chapel at St. Luke's Methodist Church Saturday, July 18, 1969. Janie was attended by her sisters, Sally and Blake Ford and I was attended by my brother David and longtime Lufkin friend Robert B. "Butch" McEntire. Our reception was a beautiful affair at the Houston Country Club, after which we spent our first night of marriage at the Warwick Hotel. The next morning, Judy and John Hutchison came by and shuttled us to the airport for an early flight to Jamaica. What an exhausting week, and what an amazing job Janie and her mom did pulling it all together!

Our honeymoon was memorable for several reasons. Our flight was packed, and we were unable to sit together, despite our pleas to other passengers. When we arrived in Montego Bay, Janie's suitcase containing her carefully selected trousseau was missing and was never recovered. I even insisted on climbing up into our plane's cargo hold to search, but to no avail. All she had to wear for the daily activities, buffets, and evening parties at the Jamaica Hilton was the long-sleeved, tailored dress she wore on the plane and a bathing suit. We took a taxi into the village of Ocho Rios to shop, but there was some national holiday going on, and all shops were closed. We finally were able to purchase some slacks and a blouse at the hotel gift shop, which had been closed for inventory until our last day. We booked a marlin fishing trip one day, but the seas were rough, and Janie developed a terrible migraine with nausea and was very ill by the time we returned and for the majority of our remaining honeymoon. We watched Neil Armstrong walk on the moon on July 20 on our room TV. On our trip back to Montego Bay for our flight home, we were amazed at how excited the Jamaicans were about the whole mission. It was as if it was their very own, and their joy made us really proud to be Americans.

The day after our return to Houston, we rented a small U-Haul trailer, packed it with our meager belongings and wedding gifts, hooked it up to Janie's 1967 Camaro, said our fond farewells, and headed off to Augusta. In the car, we packed some clothes and a cat box for Janie's beloved cat. Janie had adopted Buffy, a pretty yellow female kitten from the animal shelter in Austin. She got the cat before she got me. I had never been a cat lover but decided I'd better get used to Buffy. I grew to love her, too, and we had her for nineteen and one-half years. She was very intelligent and long suffering through ten moves and the childhood years of our three daughters.

Ft. Gordon, Georgia

Unfortunately, our new home in Augusta had a no-pets policy. Buffy was well trained to a cat box, and kept her head down as long as we were home, but when we were gone, it seems she would park herself on the windowsill and watch the world go by. She knew that was a no-no and would jump down when she saw us approaching, so we were somewhat surprised when we got our eviction notice. By this time, Janie was pregnant, and it was very inconvenient to have to find a new domicile and move on short notice. We did locate a nice little rent house, and the move worked out fine, although we hated to leave our great neighbors, Cleve and Nancy Collins. He was in medical school back then and they are now retired and living in Helotes, Texas. We still remain in touch.

Other good friends were neighbors Frank and Becky Hill; Les and Faye Burbage; my boss Leo Eandiorio and his wife Pia; and Gary and Terri Mills. Gary and I had become friends at Ft. Sam Houston, and he got assigned to the hospital at Ft. Gordon. We also were fond of Jimmy and Sally Curtis. Jimmy was an MSC at the hospital and had just returned from Vietnam where he served with the 95th Evacuation Hospital in Da Nang. Unfortunately, we have lost contact with almost all of our Army friends over the years.

Our first two years at Ft. Gordon were quite pleasant, and moving off to the great unknown as newly-weds actually strengthened our marriage, for we were forced to rely totally on each other and make all new friends. I quickly settled into my new job, which was pretty much an eight-to-five, low-stress occupation. Ft. Gordon, in addition to being a primary home to the Military Police and Signal Corps and their trainees, was a specialized training center, meaning basic training and advanced infantry training were a main focus. We provided dental services for thousands of troops and their dependents. Our facilities consisted of four WWII-era, two-story barracks buildings, the administrative offices and a small supply building. Staffing consisted of forty-five to fifty dentists, about 100 enlisted assistants, about four NCOs, and me. I was the designated supply officer, and my primary duty there seemed to be loss prevention of dental handpieces (drills). We had hundreds of them, and they were quite valuable and small and seemed to disappear easily. I also maintained a duty roster which mandated which dentist was confined to the post to handle dental emergencies on weekends and holidays. I endured many heated discussions with officers who outranked me about my math skills in maintaining an unbiased rotation, but the numbers never lied.

Janie quickly settled into being an army wife. Even though we became pregnant about four months after our marriage, she became an active member of the Officer's Wives Club and several of their benevolent endeavors. She was selected as first runner-up in the Mrs. Lieutenant contest for all the lieutenant wives at Ft. Gordon. That was a pretty big deal and widely publicized throughout the post.

Of course, it greatly pleased my boss and all the field grade career officers in the dental service. The older colonels loved flirting with the cute young lieutenant's wife, and Janie handled them beautifully. She had just completed her provisional requirements into the

Junior League of Houston prior to moving to Augusta, and she was rapidly accepted by the Jr. League there. I didn't know much about it, but learned quickly that it was quite an honor. Their big annual fundraiser was "The Follies." Now, I was newly married and hadn't seen this side of my bride, yet. I found I was volunteered to do a professionally choreographed dance number with my pregnant wife and several other couples. The men were all decked out in seersucker sport coats, pink ties, spats, straw hats, and canes. The women were dressed in Southern ball gowns, big hats, and parasols. As it turned out, Mamie Eisenhower was in town (she and the former President owned a cabin on the Augusta National Golf Course) and was seated in the first row. The next morning, there was a picture of Janie and me on the front page of the Augusta newspaper doing our dance routine in front of the First Lady. I sure hoped none of my squirrel huntin', bass fishin' buddies took that paper.

As with most things military, there was competition among the various branches and commands, "Mrs. Lt." being just one example. Another was the post softball league. Although the Dental Unit command was attached to the hospital, we both fielded our own teams. But the hospital team was predominantly the best softball team at Ft. Gordon, much to the chagrin of the other branches. The obvious reasons, at least to me, were the large base of more mature players (doctors) and an extremely talented pitcher, a senior NCO (noncommissioned officer; a sergeant) whose primary assignment was apparently to ensure that the hospital commander maintained his uninterrupted collection of Ft. Gordon softball champion trophies. The rumor was that he had been stationed at Ft. Gordon for more than six years when three-plus years was considered a long-duty assignment for any NCO or junior officer. Go figure.

My previous ball playing career was limited to about three years of Little League. I was scrawny and asthmatic as an eight-year-old and probably intimidated by all the surrounding bigger kids, so I never developed much self-confidence. The Army changed all that; I was encouraged (expected) to play with my unit. As it turns out, I apparently was a late bloomer and became our starting pitcher and even batted clean-up. The full story was that no one on our team had fast-pitch softball skills, and I could at least pitch strikes at a reasonable speed, so I became our pitcher, much to the delight of all opposing batters.

I became our number four batter because I was a pretty fair hitter, although seldom did I reach the outfield. The strategy there was that our number-three hitter, a dentist by the name of Foushee, had blazing speed and beat out a lot of ground balls. If I got any kind of hit, he could almost round two bases before I could reach first. Anyway, we stayed competitive in the league, I gained some weight, and I grew to really love softball and played for several years.

The Ft. Gordon hospital, officially named U.S. Army Hospital Specialized Treatment Center, was constructed during WWII. It was one story and was all white-painted lumber construction. It surprisingly had over 1,000 beds, its hallways were at least a mile long, and it covered many acres. The birth there of our daughter Shannon was another new experience in the world of military life. The rolled linoleum floors, whitewashed walls, and open wards (no private rooms that we ever saw) were less than inviting. Janie was in labor for over fourteen hours while I sat in a tiny waiting room on old vinyl-covered kitchen chairs. My only update was when a nurse came to inform me that I was now a father. After delivering, Janie was rolled into a recovery ward and kept flat on her back for about six hours to prevent anesthesia-induced migraines. Sadly, the young woman in the next bed had lost her baby and was very distraught, making it difficult for Janie to experience the excitement of a new baby girl. Post recovery, Janie was rolled into an open ward with several other mothers for the night. The next morning, the mothers were required to change their sheets, then walk down a hall to enjoy their breakfast sitting at picnic-style tables. Next, they walked back down the halls to retrieve their newborns and take them back to their beds for nursing. No sissy wheelchairs for those women! I think Janie was there for two more days before being discharged. I wondered if President Nixon might have received a finger shaking complaint letter from Janie's mom. But, hey, this was the Army, and our total cost was only $5.85. Plus, did I mention the winning hospital softball team?

***

The little house we rented worked out well for us, and Janie's nesting instincts proved to be very strong as we ended up painting the whole interior and fixing everything in sight. Surely, we were the best renters the owners ever had. Fortunately, we had a month-to-month lease because within a week of Shannon's birth, we were notified that an on-base apartment in the officers housing area had come open, and we had about two days to decide if we wanted to rent it. It was larger, newer, cheaper, Army maintained, and convenient to everything. Therefore, we grabbed it, even though we had to pack up all we owned along with our new baby and move again. Ah, youth!

I got a huge raise when I joined the Army compared to my teaching salary, and certainly our living quarters were now quite nice. On my one-year anniversary, I was promoted to First Lieutenant. Life was good, and my duties were quite unremarkable. Then, the whole medical situation at Ft. Gordon and probably the entire Army got reorganized. The U.S. Army Hospital Specialized Treatment Center was changed to Headquarters U.S. Army Medical Department Activity, Ft. Gordon, GA (MEDDAC). Our organization was changed from U.S. Army Dental Unit to Dental Company, MEDDAC. Our 100 enlisted personnel became Dental Detachment, and I became their Commanding Officer. I kept all my previous duties such as Property Book Officer, Voting Officer, Maintenance Officer, Postal Officer, Safety Officer, Security Control Officer, Assistant Fire Marshal, Savings Officer, custodian of company unit fund, Reenlistment Officer, Class A Agent for Disbursements Officer, and a few others. I don't remember the duties any of them entailed except for Savings Officer. I had to make the rounds of the dental clinics every so often trying to sell U.S. savings bonds to help support our war efforts. That was really a tough sell, especially to the dentists.

My new duties were primarily command in nature, such as some rare drill and ceremony, barracks inspections, and disciplinary judgments (Article 15 jurisdiction over enlisted personnel). As was the typical Army way, I received almost no training for any of my duties, so I leaned heavily on my sergeants for explanation and advice. There were also reams of regulations available to explain everything, but no one seemed to have time to study them and interpret the military jargon. Really boring stuff! However, looking back, the Army played a major role in developing my people skills and problem-solving abilities. Once I learned that the Army was not interested in excuses, but solutions, I thrived much better, and in July 1971 was awarded the Army Commendation Medal for my efforts in helping the restructuring of Ft. Gordon's dental company.

In May 1971, I was promoted to Captain. This seemed to be a milestone because it marked the final year of my three-year commitment to the Army.

Typically, no one who had less than twelve months left to serve was ordered to Vietnam. Janie and I thought we had dodged that assignment and could now breathe a sigh of relief. I can still recall the exact words from Maj. Damian, the Adjutant of MEDDAC, when he called me in July. "Jim, I'm afraid I've got some bad news for you. You just got orders for Nam." I had only eight months left to serve! Rapidly, Janie and I began gearing ourselves up to dismantle our lives in preparation for moving back to Houston while I began training for Vietnam. I also got three more vaccines in addition to the fourteen I had received at Ft. Sam Houston.

Training for War

All medical service officers with Vietnam assignments were required to undergo familiarization with the M16 rifle. I actually went on to earn the expert badge with rifle bar. I just happened to find the awarding order while researching these memoirs. I never received the badge and didn't remember that I had qualified for it. I was subsequently designated as a range officer and given the responsibility of M16 familiarization for all MEDDAC officers headed for Nam. I grew up around guns and was comfortable with all the safety issues that accompanied them. However, lining up twenty officers to shoot fully automatic rifles when many of them had never touched a lethal weapon of any kind created its own set of safety concerns.

After the perfunctory lectures on the weapon, how to aim it, and the basics of gun safety, each officer was assigned his spot in a long trench from which all would be shooting at their individual target downrange. There were a couple of NCOs stationed along the back of the trench assisting the shooters and then the Range Officer (me) and a senior NCO with a microphone were stationed in a tower directly over the trench with a view of all shooters—approximately ten to our right and ten to our left. Initial firing was single shots, then three quick shots on semi-automatic. That went pretty well, but there was a physician captain immediately below our tower who must have been in the throes of a panic attack. The next command was for three shot bursts on fully automatic. When I gave the command, "Ready on the right, ready on the left, commence firing," he pointed his M16 down range, closed his eyes, and pulled the trigger. By the time his magazine was emptied, the recoil of twenty rounds had left his rifle pointing straight up with my NCO and I hugging each other against the back wall of the tower. It was very scary and happened so fast all any of us could do was duck. The next commands were "Cease fire, disarm that s.o.b. and get his ass out of the trench!" I don't know what happened to the captain, but I assume he was given credit for M16 familiarization and got sent on his way to Nam.

I enjoyed my time at Ft. Gordon. That was an exciting period in our lives with many unknowns and new experiences. Almost everything I did was on-the-job training, but that was apparently the main function of young MSC officers, to just handle the jobs that were thrown at them. Figure it out. I did get to do some fishing with Gary Mills on some of the backwater swamps on the fort and also on Clark Hill Reservoir outside of Augusta, and I also killed a buck while hunting some of the old artillery ranges that comprised much of the land. There were old shells and shrapnel everywhere on Ft. Gordon's artillery ranges. I also found a few arrowheads, most of which were white quartz. I came across several old whiskey stills on the Fort land, which reminds me of present day marijuana farms that are frequently planted on Federal lands to avoid leaving an ownership trail.

I regret not staying in touch with our friends we made there—Leo and Pia Eandiorio and Gary and Terri Mills, especially. Everyone has regrets, but I've learned that life is largely a parade of people who pass through our lives and help make us who we are.

We loaded up at the end of July 1971, bid Georgia farewell,

and headed back to Houston. I was granted a month's leave, so Janie and Shannon could get settled in with Janie's parents while I was still around. Saying goodbye to my dear wife and one-year-old daughter was the hardest thing I will probably ever do. Knowing Shannon would learn to walk and talk while I was gone was incredibly painful, not to mention the dark and unspoken possibility that I might not even come back. Janie could not bring herself to drop me off at the Houston International Airport, so my dear, Lufkin friend, R.B. "Butch" McIntire agreed to take me that morning.

I caught a flight to San Francisco, then boarded a military bus that transported a bunch of us to Travis Air force Base near Oakland. It was a very somber trip for all aboard, since none of us seemed to know anyone else on the bus nor the commercial airliner we boarded for the flight to Nam.

Arrival and Letters Home from Vietnam
September 1971

In the following letters home there are various ethnic terms that were used in the 1960s and 70s. None are meant to be disparaging. Only one was disrespectful, and that is the term "gooks" in reference to the North Vietnamese and Viet Cong who were trying to kill me and every other American. They were the terms of the day. All Veterans reading this historic narrative will understand.

From this juncture, comments within quotation marks are from my letters home. Comments not within quotation marks are additional explanations.

> SEPT 1, 1971, Via post card: "26 hours from Houston and still 4 hours to go. Stop overs in Honolulu and Okinawa. 168 of us (mostly officers and senior enlisted) on an American Airlines 707. We are all very tired."

It was about midday when we flew over the coast, and I recall uneasiness as the jet slowed and things below began to come into focus. I vividly remember seeing thousands of circular spots that I could only assume were bomb and artillery craters, and my predominant thought was, *I don't think I'm going to like this place very much.*

We landed at Bien Hoa Air Base just outside Saigon. I suppose all newbies processed through the personnel facilities there. As we taxied to a stop, the flight attendant, who was probably about the age of our mothers, came on her mic, pointed out a hangar-style building, and directed us to double-time into it when we disembarked due to concerns over snipers. Stepping off the plane, I remember being accosted by an overwhelming sensory assault of the noise of helicopters, Skyraider fighter planes, jets, and diesel vehicles along with the smells of aviation fuel, and just as we had been warned in our stateside indoctrination, the smell of burning shit. We soon learned that flush toilets were rare, therefore most toilet facilities were latrines. Fifty-five-gallon drums caught the waste under the two-holers and when full, they were picked up by "hump squads," trucked to designated locations, and incinerated with diesel fuel. The stink seemed to permeate the entire country.

> SEPT 2. "We finally arrived in Bien Hoa at 10:00 AM. It is now 5:20 PM and has begun to cool off some. All our baggage got rained on earlier today so most of my things are wet. If my writing seems bad it is because I'm sitting on a sandbag in front of my sleeping quarters trying to keep the flies off me. I was very depressed when we first landed and even more so on the bus ride from Bien Hoa to Long Binh. Everything is ratty and temporary. There are no trees on the base; watch towers and barbed wire and helicopters are everywhere. I can't remember ever being so tired. Tomorrow morning, I should find out what my assignment will be. I am presently at a transient replacement battalion

in Long Binh. We are all waiting for assignments or flights to assignments. Most of the bases seem to be on alert due to increased actions generated by the elections. I'm sorry this letter is so short. I had a lot of things I wanted to say, but they all sound the same, I'm afraid (depression and despair), and all I can think about at the moment is finally having a place to stretch out, even if it is hot and muggy. By the way, we are 11 hours ahead of Houston."

While at Long Binh, we were given our new uniforms, as I recall, two or three sets of fatigues, a pair of jungle boots, and some olive drab T-shirts and boxer shorts with a duffel bag to put it all in. We had each been allowed to bring a small suitcase of toiletries and some underwear, and most had been in their khakis the entire trip. I think we had to take our new fatigues to a Vietnamese shop to have our name, rank, branch, and insignia patches sewn on.

"This replacement station is every inch the hole Jimmy Curtis said it was. The sheds we sleep in hold about 40 men each, double bunked. I doubt the mattresses have ever been sunned. The outside walls are sand bagged so there is no breeze. It's too hot to sleep during the day and we are restricted to this area, so about all there is to do is go to the Officers' Club and drink beer."

I found it tiny, dark, and crowded with guys I didn't know getting drunk. Not my deal. I went back to my assigned barracks and read a book I had bought in the San Francisco airport. It had caught my attention because it pictured a guy pulling a bow and arrow on the cover. It was *Deliverance*. Not what could be called a feel-good mood elevator. It was unbearably hot all day and the smell of sweat, urine and vomit was overwhelming. We just lay in our sweat under mosquito nets until we fell asleep from fatigue or too many beers. Welcome to Nam.

SEPT 3. "The drug program is the big thing here now. It gets first priority on all incoming medical personnel. I don't think I want into that. I'm a little anxious about what kind of job I will get up north. The letter Col. McCall wrote seems to have had a really good job lined up for me at Bien Hoa, but the personnel officer got me confused with a captain who had my job at Ft. Campbell. Anyway, he got the job and I am in the melting pot still."

I was relieved to finally see my name on a list to board a C-130 headed to Da Nang. That was about a 2-hour flight on the loudest and most uncomfortable airplane I ever flew on. Upon landing, I was picked up and delivered to the 95th Evacuation Hospital. That was nice. The 95th was built on this site in 1968 and had about 320 air-conditioned beds in white single-story wings. It was able to provide neurologic, dermatologic, psychiatric, and radiologic services, as well as almost all surgical specialties. I remember feeling better about things there. These were "my people."

SEPT 6. "I am now in Da Nang and just processed through the personnel shop Jimmy Curtis used to be in charge of. Six of us arrived together and spent last night in a ward at the 95th Evac. It was wonderful. Air conditioned and clean sheets!"

Letters Home from 85th Evacuation Hospital Vietnam, 1971

I remember Jimmy telling me most Captain MSC assignments would be pretty good for the most part, and the only one I should really try to avoid was the 85th. It was the pits.

"Jimmy's friend who replaced him, and who Jimmy promised would give me a good job, left yesterday for 14 days leave in the States, so I never got to talk to him.

I fly out of here by chopper tomorrow morning for Phu Bai and the 85th Evac. It is a 100-bed hospital, and I will probably be adjutant and detachment commander from what they've told me here. My address will be the same as on this envelope. Hopefully you will have gotten it by telegram before you get this letter.

What new tricks can Shannon do now? I can honestly only now begin to let myself even think about her. I don't think anything has ever so deeply upset me as when I had to walk out of her room that last time. This all seems so useless and senseless. I must say tho, that we do appear to be pulling out pretty quickly, tho I'm sure it won't bring me home any earlier. No medical facilities are left except the larger hospitals, with a few exceptions. I may even see the close down of the hospital I'm going to.

I heard that letters take about 7 days to reach the U.S., but only about 3 to reach Nam—figure that one out. I'm really looking forward to hearing from you. I know this isn't easy for you either. I love you, darling. Please get a kiss from Shannon for me.

The next day, I caught a ride on a Huey with a Colonel who was the CO (commanding officer) of the 67th Medical Group, which is responsible for all medical activities for the northern sector of Nam. We flew to Quảng Trị, which is the northern most U.S. base, just below the DMZ (Demilitarized Zone, the boundary between North and South Vietnam). There was an aid station there, and the Col. wanted to check the damage from a rocket attack the previous day. There were several damaged buildings and a lot of smoke still, but I don't think anyone got injured. I quickly determined the first order of business upon landing in new territory is to learn where the closest bunker is. From there we flew back down to Phu Bai and landed at the 85th helipad."

The official designation of my new home was 85th Evacuation Hospital, SMBL. The acronym of SMBL stands for "Semi-Mobile." That meant that we had (or should have) the capability to load up and move the entire hospital within twenty-four hours. Therefore, we had a few trucks assigned to us and maintained on our campus. Several of the hospitals in Nam were SMBLs. This contrasts with MASH units (Mobile Army Surgical Hospitals) that moved frequently in Korea to stay close to the action.

The mention of MASH units reminds me that there were maybe two movie theaters at Ft. Gordon that typically showed latest releases with tickets discounted for Soldiers. I remember there being lots of complaints when the Army banned the showing of *M*A*S*H* at its post theaters. It was one of the top grossing films in 1970, but it was apparently deemed a thinly veiled slam on America's involvement in

Vietnam. Of course, that made it even more of a "must-see" for all the soldiers. The 2nd MASH Unit served in Nam only from October 1966 to July 1967 before being replaced by SMBL evacuation hospitals as the war expanded. The advent of dustoffs allowed casualties to be transferred rapidly to the better equipped evacuation hospitals.

Medivac choppers were known universally as dustoffs. They swoop down, get wounded loaded on, and are gone quickly, usually in a cloud of dust. They have large red crosses painted on them and are not armed, as opposed to the "slicks," which are the same type chopper (UH-1 or Huey) and which frequently had M60 machine guns mounted at each side door. We often had patients brought in by slicks, which frequently was an indication of a "hot pickup" (under fire).

All established helipads were made of Perforated Steel Planks (PSPs). The planks could be snapped together and could create rapid paving for roads and landing pads (as well as footpaths to our latrines). Ours had "Phu Bai Dust Off 47.40" painted on its surface in large white letters. The numbers were our radio frequency so that any chopper could communicate its landing intentions if they needed immediate assistance. Unannounced ships were not appreciated.

The term "chopper" originated with helicopters in Korea due to the distinct chopping sound their big blades made in flight, especially during lift off and sharp turns. The term became generic for all helicopters, but be assured that every veteran of Vietnam can still identify the sound of a Huey among any other aircraft.

SEPT 8. "Phu Bai is about 50 miles north of Da Nang and is the base camp for the 2nd Brigade, 101st Airborne Division. The 101st are the northernmost U.S. ground forces and our protectors here at the hospital. I think this is a pretty safe place to be, as we treat a lot of Viet Cong (VC) and also a few North Vietnamese Army. (NVA) prisoners, so they are not apt to shell us. More about this later. Our perimeter is constantly patrolled by the 101st and the hospital is next to an airbase which houses about 400 aircraft, including 100 Cobra gunships. The 101st is expected to leave within a year and I've been told the VC and NVA seem to have taken the attitude that there will be less wear and tear on everyone if they leave us alone and let us leave. With all the firepower around here, I think I would too."

I saw on a documentary that the NVA took control of Phu Bai and its surroundings as soon as April 1972, shortly after the 101st and the 85th pulled out.

Letters Home from 85th Evacuation Hospital Vietnam, 1971

Overhead view of the 85th Evac Hospital

1. Emergency Room and Admissions and Disposition Office and Communications Center
2. Operating Room and Intensive Care (ICU)
3. Wards 1, 2, and 3. Diseases and Drug Treatments
4. Unknown
5. Ward 5. Orthopedics and Trauma
6. Registrar Office
7. Helipad
8. Mess Hall
9. Enlisted Men's Club
10. My Hooch – home sweet home
11. Supply. Also has small gym fixed up in rear portion. Former airplane hangar.
12. Hospital Headquarters
13. Officers and Non-Commissioned Officers Quarters
14. Female Nurses Quarters
15. Enlisted Men Quarters
16. Officers Club
17. Highway 1. Runs almost entire length of Vietnam
18. Da Nang-Hue Railroad. "Most dangerous railroad in the World." Runs through Hai Van Pass.
19. Revetments (protected slots) where intelligence gathering planes are parked
20. Motor Pool and Medical Supply Warehouse

Letters Home from 85th Evacuation Hospital Vietnam, 1971

The Phu Bai/Hue landing strip can be seen just above the hospital. The dark blocks beyond the runway are protective barriers within which helicopters are parked. Several Chinooks (CH-47) can be seen parked in upper left corner.

"This place is much worse than I ever expected. It seems to be an old temporary Marine hospital built a few years ago. The latrines are little 2 holers and we have no hot water for shaving. Everything possible was built on stilts because we are in the heart of the monsoon area. They begin about the first of October and last 6 months and it rains every day, supposedly. I hope that isn't true. Phu Bai is on the coastal plain, not far from the ocean. There is a line of hills about 2 miles behind us and beyond that a mountain range about as high or higher than the Smokies, but more jagged. I've been surprised at how rough these mountains are around here.

Honey, I'm thankful you are staying with your folks. You sounded as tho you were having a pretty bad time of it on the phone and I'm sure it would really get bad if you were by yourself. [I must have called home from Biên Hòa or possibly the 95th.] I don't think I'll have too many chances to call. They say the MARS (radio) calls get bad reception from here. I'll probably call that way next time, tho. Let me know how much the phone call was so I will know which way may be the best. I had to wait about three hours, between standing in line and trying to get the call through. Hopefully it won't always be that bad. I had given up and gone to bed at 10:00 pm since the operators go home at 10, but I guess they felt sorry for us. Anyway, the Sgt. who was on before me had tried to get a line through for an hour (it's in a small, soundproof room, about 85 degrees). He got through right after I left and then came and got me, so I thanked him diligently. We can only call from here on Tuesday nights, from 8 until 10, 5 minute limits, so it will probably be Tuesday mornings there between 7 and 9. I don't know when I'll be able to get a tape recorder, as the PX (Post Exchange) here is not well stocked at all."

The MARS system required a radio operator to mediate between the two callers. As one finished his comments, he or she would announce "over," and the other caller could respond and finish with another "over." It was extremely awkward to have a personal conversation and was also cost prohibitive.

"As for my job, I am the Adjutant (administrative assistant to the senior officers). It looks as though I will be very busy, as I have many other incidental jobs due to a shortage of MSCs. I think there are about 8 of us, only one of which is a Lt., and one a Maj., our Executive Officer (XO - second in command). The rest are Captains. The hospital Commanding Officer (CO) is a Lieutenant Colonel and a physician. In all I think we have about 100 officers, most of whom are physicians or nurses and about 190 enlisted, most of whom are medics."

My first afternoon as Adjutant, I accompanied the hospital CO and XO to a security briefing at the 101st HQ. Until then I had wondered why the Army required a "Secret" security clearance for officers headed for Nam. It seemed strange that the FBI had been in Lufkin asking lifelong acquaintances about me. That was an extremely interesting and enlightening briefing and I remember being stunned at how many NVA units were known to be nearby. It also explained why the "whump" of mortars being fired by our guys could be heard frequently throughout many nights.

> "My quarters consist of a little house with a tin roof. It looks like a chicken house since its on stilts. It (and all of our other hooches) has two rooms. The other room is occupied by a colored MSC captain, George Bodie, who got here a week before I did."

I never mentioned in my letters that there was a bullet hole through my hooch mate's door that passed through our common wall and exited through my back wall. I was told that about two weeks earlier, a Soldier with an M16 shot and killed another guy standing on the stoop. We all deduced it probably involved drugs.

> "The hospital is next to the small airbase so it is very noisy here. I think it would be impossible to count less than 6 choppers in the air at any one time within a half mile radius."

SEPT 9. "Well, I got fired today. Actually, a new captain with better qualifications arrived, so I was changed to Assistant Registrar. The registrar leaves in a couple of months, so actually I am training to take his place. I think I will like it much better than the adjutant job anyway. I wasn't especially fond of our Executive Officer with whom I shared an office. I will be working more in the hospital, which is air conditioned and should be more interesting, too.

There is a terrific drug problem at the hospital. A lot of the enlisted men are "skag freaks" (heroin addicts) and several overdoses are treated every week. In fact, one died last night. The heroin is so pure here (95% as opposed to 5% in the U.S.), that guys are hooked and overdose before they know what happened."

Actually, when I tried to put on my newly issued galoshes, I was impeded by a sandwich bag full of marijuana stuffed in the toe. The hospital grounds were littered with empty plastic bubbles, the kind that were used in candy and gum machines in the U.S. In Nam, they were used to contain "nickel hits," five dollars' worth of heroin. Our housekeeping and clothes washing was done by "mama-sans," Vietnamese women who were admitted each morning through our front gate. I think they were searched or at least maybe dog checked, but once they were in, the druggies could easily arrange a heroin purchase for that night. Some of our perimeter spotlights were always out due to our own guards breaking them so mama-sans or their dealers could throw drink cans containing heroin over the fence.

"Please don't worry about me, as I am in very little danger. It's just hard to be in a place where no one else wants to be."

Letters Home from 85th Evacuation Hospital Vietnam, 1971

"Home, sweet home." My hooch. I lived in the left side of the hooch. The roof was later sandbagged after Typhoon Hester hit. Tires seen here didn't help much.

"The Ghetto." Enlisted men's quarters. Notice protective sand filled barrels and sandbags. Bunker is to the right.

Sept 10. "Well, today hasn't been very exciting. I spent this morning studying regulations and learning how to fill out medivac forms. I will start off being the A&D (admissions and dispositions) Officer. I'll work in the emergency room and oversee the administrative end of admitting patients. I'm also being taught to coordinate medivac flights to larger hospitals (Japan, Philippines, Okinawa, etc.) and the U.S. You'd be surprised how many patients we send to Ft. Gordon.

I have still not been able to process thru finance yet. It will be best if you can live on what we have in savings, though, as I still want to deposit all I can here at 10%

interest. My salary is $1006.00 per month. Just for your information, we work from 7:30 to 5:30 as official duty hours, although Bill Green, our registrar, seems to work longer and says I will, too. Also, I come up on AOD (Administrative Officer of the Day) next week for the first time. I get to go to bed at 12:30 AM, but am subject to call at any time due to very seriously ill admissions, deaths, medivacs, and breeches in perimeter security. As for the temperature here, it runs up to around 100 degrees most days, although due to the humidity, I sweat like crazy and take 2-4 salt tablets daily.

I am hoping to get your first letter tomorrow. It seems like we've been separated for more than just a week and a half."

My first day as A&D Officer was quite an eye opener. I think it was probably our senior NCO, Staff Sgt. McLemore who gave me the tour and familiarization. Our first stop was the "dead shed." It was a small tin roof shed, and Sgt. Mc stressed how secure it was to be kept at all times as he handed me the key. Upon unlocking the door, on the cement floor was the head and left shoulder of a Soldier as well as his tibia broken off in his boot. That was all that could be found of him. I will not ever be able to unsee him, as I had hardly ever been to a funeral at my young age (twenty-four) and had certainly never seen a dead person at my feet. Apparently, he was attempting to disarm a mine. Medivacs (usually just called dustoffs) occasionally delivered KIAs, (Killed in Action) along with wounded, and those bodies were placed in the shed for pickup by Graves Registration personnel.

The next stop was within a few feet. It was the Ordinance Bunker, a small building made from concrete-covered sandbags. Another of my new responsibilities was to ensure that no explosive devises entered our hospital. Severely wounded men were frequently raced from their dustoffs on gurneys and straight into the ER still in their rucksacks and with ammunition, grenades and/or claymore antipersonnel mines still strapped on them. Typically, it fell to A&D personnel to remove all those prior to entry and then deposit them in the ordinance bunker ASAP. Neither I nor any of my four men had training with such matters, so I was always apprehensive when those items were frantically dropped to the concrete floor as uniforms were being cut away.

Upon entering the hospital, the actual ER was immediately on the right and consisted of five pipe frames onto which patients on litters were transferred from the waist-high gurneys. Overhead piping provided oxygen hookups and IV hangers. At the far end of the room hung a large water hose which was used to wash away the blood, tissue, and other debris that missed the stainless-steel buckets during trauma procedures.

A&D was to the left. It had a counter behind which worked one to three men whose job was to collect information about and belongings of each patient. The wounded's unit usually knew we had him and would send a representative, but in the interim, his belongings were cataloged and secured in one of many small cubicles that covered our back wall where they could be closely watched by our guys.

Entrance to Emergency Room at 85th Evac.

SEPT 11. "Yea! I finally received your letter today. It was so good to hear from you and know what you were thinking plus all the news. I went out and bought the only cassette recorder the PX had today. Don't know when I'll get a tape off though, as they didn't have any cassettes – soon though. $48. I only got paid today so this was the first time I could buy anything.

You asked about entertainment – there's very little. We got our projector fixed for the first time in a month last night and they showed *Psycho*. I didn't even watch it. Tonight, a floor show is coming to our rinky-dink officer's club. I usually read some, but by the time I finish work, eat, shower, write you and have a beer, its bedtime. So far, I've read half of *Airport* (but gave it up as a lost cause), *The Inheritors, and Deliverance*. Now I'm reading *The Andromeda Strain* and like it really well.

The "Dead Shed" where bodies were secured until Graves Registration could pick them up. Gurneys were also stored here and rolled out to choppers when patients were brought in, usually on litters (stretchers.) To the left is the ordinance bunker where ammo, grenades, and claymore mines were secured after clearing off from wounded soldiers.

Emergency Room at 85th. Patients brought in on litters were placed on the pipe racks. Clothes were cut off and dropped in buckets beside each rack along with bandages that had been applied in the field or on the chopper. IVs were hung from a yellow pipe suspended along the ceiling. Note water hose coiled on the back wall for washing down the floor.

Dear Janie

Spec.4 Jerry Dodd, RTO (radio operator,) a very dependable and important team member. Map of the northern sector on the wall was critical for tracking ETAs of incoming dustoffs to alert trauma teams. The radio room was adjacent to the ER.

"I haven't made any close friends so far. I like all the MSCs quite well, except the XO and the new adjutant. They're too "strac" (regular Army; career) and take everything very seriously. The rest of us seem more relaxed and take things as they come. I especially like Ted Becker. He has a master's in fisheries biology and has worked for N. Dakota and Montana Game and Fish Departments. He is our Supply Officer and a real character.

We had something like a horrible nightmare today. A GI was brought in that was so messed up I gagged when I saw and smelled him. Most of his clothes were burned off and his face and chest were black and still smoking and burning. An acquaintance riding in the back of a truck had thrown a white phosphorus (WP) grenade towards him, thinking it was a smoke grenade. It happened just down the road from the hospital. WP, also called "Willie Pete," is impossible to extinguish and burns until it burns itself out. The stench is still all over the ER 8 hours later. The guy with him got his face burned terribly and I imagine both will be blind (if they live). His buddy still had WP in his eyes and when they were pried open smoke came out and the nurses would dab away the WP with Q-tips and irrigate with potassium permanganate. We air evaced them to Da Nang as soon as they had IVs going and all the WP off. I'll never forget that as long as I live. The guy who tossed the grenade got his hands burned, but not badly, and the MPs took him away. It was all just senseless 18-year-old horseplay.

We were quite busy today with several battle casualties (BC), one of which was DOA (Dead on Arrival). We sort of go in spurts in admissions, most of the time doing routine sick calls and handling Vietnamese civilians, but if there is fighting in our area, we are really busy. We are not very far from Hue [pronounced "whay"], which has a large Vietnamese hospital which takes care of most of the ARVN (Army of Republic of Vietnam, South Vietnamese Army) casualties."

While five to six casualties were a fairly busy day for us, I heard that in the previous years of larger combat operations, the 85th had worked up to thirty-six hours straight to treat all the wounded. I was told that stretchers were lined up out onto our helipad during those times. That is hard to fathom, but not surprising in the least that our dedicated staff would do whatever it took.

"Tomorrow is Sunday and I only have to work 8:30 to 3:30 so hope to go to Camp Hochmuth (101st base camp) and play some tennis. I took my malaria pill today (causes mild diarrhea) and must run to the latrine – 150 yards away, so will close now. Give Shannon a long silent hug for me."

SEPT 12. "You asked about being in an evac hospital. Evacs are the primary hospitals. I think there are or were five in Nam. Some just have greater capabilities due to size and staff than the others. Of course, the size of the hospital governs its extra-curricular activities, officers' and enlisted clubs, etc., which are important distractions for all of us. I was misinformed when I said we had 100 officers and 190 enlisted. We must have only 1/2 or less of those numbers.

Phu Bai is a center for electronic intelligence gathering. In fact, most of the planes based here seem to be spy type jobs which apparently pick up electronic data and drop sensors in the jungles. I imagine anybody firing at this place would receive more return fire than he would believe. Also, our perimeters are supposedly protected by sensors. I was shown a classified film before I left Ft. Gordon that explained what is available over here and it helps our confidence to know what we have. The 101st has reconnaissance set up all around Phu Bai as well as regular night patrols. Also, each individual unit is responsible for its perimeter within the main base perimeter, and all these are manned with guards and mines each night. The hospital assigns security guards each night and our perimeter is fenced with concertina wire stretched over beds of glass from broken IV bottles."

The glass hopefully would dissuade any naked sappers (commandos trained to infiltrate our perimeters and plant explosive packs) who might try to slip through the concertina razor wire.

"I don't know which is worse, having malaria or the diarrhea the pills cause. What a life!

Today we had three booby trap victims. One had his foot, hand, and side blownoff and later died. One lost his hand and an eye, but is still alive. He's too critical to evac yet. The other was DOA. We put his head and a foot in the shed. One can't really and truly appreciate how horrible war is until they've seen it, I'm sure, because I've seen only a small fraction of what can happen without seeing battle itself. It's just very hard to put into words what you feel when you see a fellow human so mutilated and in such suffering. And I doubt that any of them could tell you exactly why he was here or for what cause he had given his future or his life. They just get drafted and go where they're sent. I really haven't heard anyone here voice their opinion of the war. I think we all feel about the same and just try not to think about it. Maybe it's easier to do that when you don't have to really lay it on the line all the time. Enough of that.

The more I get into this job the more time it consumes. I try to get over to the ER each time I hear a dustoff coming in. Seems like most land at lunch, dinner, and after 10:00 at night."

SEPT 13. "I got to take today off, which was a welcome relief. I didn't realize how nice it is to have a weekend to look forward to until I didn't have one. I slept until 9:00 but had to get up due to diarrhea. One of the docs prescribed some good pills that seem to be working well. I went to the ER about 3:00 and got put to work. The casualty was quite a coincidence because it was a pilot whose chopper had been shot down. I just met him last night and he shared a dinner table with us. We were asking him where they were making contact with the NVA. He told us about taking fire yesterday and darn if they didn't get him today. Fortunately, he only got a broken leg from the crash, especially since his wife is a nurse here.

Letters Home from 85th Evacuation Hospital Vietnam, 1971

East side guard tower overlooking the runway.

Entire hospital perimeter was enclosed by concertina wire underlaid with broken IV bottles.

I got my first haircut today. My hair gets oily and matty easily here in the humidity, so I got it thinned a little. The barber was Vietnamese. Evidently, they find excess hair unsightly because before I knew what was happening, this guy was shaving the fuzz of my earlobes. He had a real stern look, so I let him finish. Better no fuzz than no ears, and it was a pretty good haircut for 30 cents. Also, please send me an electric razor. That should be much better than wading 150 yards at 6:30 am for a cold water shave this winter."

SEPT 14. "I got your '101 ways to make love' card today. It didn't list them, unfortunately, and I can only think of 47 (ha!), but I'm anxious to try them out with you. And Happy Birthday today!"

Most of our letters began and ended with lots of terms of endearment and longings for one another. We were essentially still newlyweds and desperately missed each other, as no doubt has been happening to military couples for time immemorial. Those lovey parts of our letters have been mostly left out to spare the readers, although they were still an important aspect of our story and critical to our emotional struggles during those trying times.

"We had only one BC (battle casualty) today. He had hit a booby trap and was perforated all over his upper body with dirt and pebbles from the blast. As bad as he looked, the doc says he will live, although he might be blind. We flew him down to Da Nang to an ophthalmologist.

The people here are friendly enough, but no one goes out of their way towards anyone else. It's very strange. I would think that this would be sort of like med school or *M*A*S*H* with all the doctors and nurses and gore, but that doesn't seem to be the case. Maybe it's all the gore that sort of keeps spirits subdued. Or maybe I don't see what goes on behind the scenes."

SEPT 16. "Have I mentioned the hooch maids? There are several on the compound that come every day except Sunday and each is allowed to take 6 or 7 hooches. We pay them $5.00/month and they wash clothes, clean the rooms, iron fatigues, and polish our boots every day. That's about the only luxury we have that comes to mind."

Fatigues were dried by hanging them under the roof overhangs of our hooches. I later learned that doesn't work so well during the monsoon rains, and we all wore damp clothes all the time.

"It rained all last night and again tonight. It is physically possible to see the winter coming because every evening one can see the storms back in the mountains coming closer and becoming more severe. We have admitted very few casualties the last two days. May be the weather?

You would not believe the number of dogs on our compound. They are everywhere and the sorriest looking animals I've ever seen. Probably like Indian camp dogs used to be. They run all over chasing females (dogs) and each other. The men adopt them and when we have an outdoor movie, it is hilarious. The dogs come out in force and climb all over the seats and snarl and yelp until the movie is hardly audible. Today we treated a dog bite case and then called the vets to come get the dog for observation. We also X-rayed a scout dog. Seems we treat quite a few dogs.

Last night we admitted a guy for probable snake bite, but now the docs think it was an insect bite. The man had the thing in his sleeping bag. It woke him up and he slung it out, but it had bitten him on the elbow and eyebrow. I saw him today and he seemed to be fine, so it couldn't have been too bad of a critter. I'm just glad I don't sleep out in the boonies on the ground.

Today we admitted a Vietnamese for multiple GSWs (gunshot wounds) that was brought in by an American civilian adviser. There is a lot of secret stuff going on over here. Much of it involves mercenaries, Vietnamese spies, and even a few Americans in Hanoi posing as other nationalities. We being the northernmost hospital, they come here for treatment. They give only a name and social security number if they have it. We take what they give us and are expected not to ask further questions."

I remember one Asian patient who we were fairly certain was Taiwanese. He was over six feet tall and clearly was not Vietnamese. His presence in the hospital was problematic because Taiwanese supposedly were not involved in the war (tensions today are still high between Taiwan and China. Communist China was a major ally of North Vietnam). Our secret patient would have been of great interest to our enemy. Our CO, XO, and I met and finally decided to log him in under a common Vietnamese name and hope he would not be noticed by any prying eyes among our local helpers. There was a secret communications operations center with lots of antennas on a mountain overlooking Phu Bai (8th Radio Research Field Station), and we figured that's where he came from. As I recall, he was accompanied by an American, but we still were kept in the dark. We performed an appendectomy on him and sent him on his way ASAP! One of the duties of our Registrar Office was to determine as best we could who these patients worked for and bill them.

> SEPT 17. "I got 2 letters today and was really thrilled. We have 2 mail calls each day and I got one at each. Since I didn't get any the last two days, that meant four mail calls with nothing and I was really down.
>
> Casualties have really slacked off lately. We did get a Marine pilot today who had been shot in the shoulder while flying over the DMZ. Also got a guy with a broken back. He seemed to be in more pain than any patient I've seen so far.
>
> We get mail 7 days a week, so please keep writing, Darling. Also, tape a fair amount of Shannon, even if it's just her crying. It may be hard to believe, but I'm already having trouble remembering things about her, so send me lots of sounds and pictures."

SEPT 18. "As for coming home early, yes there is a very slight chance. I think it all hinges on what the 101st Airborne Division does, because we are here to support them. The rule seems to be that if your unit stands down within 90 days of the end of your release date (mine is end of April 1972), you go with them. That means we must hope the 85th closes, but not before the end of January, or I'll be reassigned over here and stay my full time.

We periodically have live floor shows at the Officers' Club and there was one last night. I went 30 min early to get a good seat and could hardly get in the door. I stood for 30 minutes drinking a hot beer (Cold beer is very rare. Ice is a treasure.) and finally left. There are 1,000 pilots based across the runway from here who live very dangerous lives and who make good money and they literally take over our club, especially when we have shows, as bad as they frequently are. I guess having nurses here makes a difference, too. The ratio of GIs to girls must be about 2,000 to 1.

I just got back from watching a movie, *Medium Cool*. We've had movies every night for a week now. I've seen *There Was a Crooked Man, Strawberry Statement, Take the Money and Run,* and *The Virgin Soldiers* and I'm glad I didn't pay to see any of them. Movies are really bad now, but they help take us away from all this for a while, anyway.

Letters Home from 85th Evacuation Hospital Vietnam, 1971

I just can't get over the number of drug freaks here. Yesterday we only admitted seven patients and three of them were for "opiate abstinence syndrome" or withdrawal symptoms. These are guys who seek amnesty. They dry out in the wards for a few days and then go to our "half-way house" to rap and supposedly help each other psychologically. They sit around most of the day and listen to rock music and get out of work, the way it looks to me. Very few make it."

Our movie theater. Note the wide screen and uncomfortable seating. Pouring rains were not appreciated.

"Ye Olde Outhouse." This is typical of latrines all over Nam. Note the PSP (planking) footpath. The trails to the latrines became terribly soggy during heavy rains.

SEPT 19. "I have AOD tonight for the first time. About all it consists of is walking the perimeter to be sure all guards are alert and that the wire is in good shape and that all vehicles are in and locked.

Today we received an ARVN interpreter who had flipped a jeep over. He complained of a sore pelvis and while in X-ray he started breathing funny. Anyway, his heart stopped, and the ER crew gave him artificial resuscitation for almost 45 minutes. Finally, it was decided he had brain damage that required that his skull be drilled into. He eventually died, for they stopped pumping his chest, at least while I was in the triage area.

The number of needless and accidental deaths over here is stunning. Yesterday, 2 GIs were brought in DOA. The ARVN night guards had neglected to disarm a claymore mine after daylight and these guys walked by and tripped it on their own helipad. We monitored a call for a dustoff yesterday and the receiver (not one of my guys) must have been new or untrained because he couldn't get the coordinates figured out and almost sent the chopper the wrong way. It was over an hour before we got the wounded guy and he was barely alive. He died on the way to Da Nang and the 95th as we don't have a neurosurgeon and he had a large head wound. That's another thing that doesn't make good sense to me. The 85th gets most of the combat casualties in the entire northern region now and yet the neurosurgeons and neurologists are 1/2 hour to 1 hour flying time away — if the choppers can even fly. I suppose they need to be centrally located, but we've heard they aren't very busy down there.

Convoys of ARVNs have been going south through here most of the evening, so either the Lom Son offensive is over, or something is building down south. Supposedly most heavy action stops until after the monsoons which seem to have started. I hear the 85th fills up with pneumonia and "fungus rot" cases during the constant rains because it's impossible to stay dry and then the weather is too bad to evac anyone. That should keep us busy.

Dear Janie

Janie, I'm so sorry I couldn't get a call to you on your birthday. This far north things aren't very civilized, so a lot of things that apply to John [husband of a friend of Janie's] just aren't the same up here. There are no nightclubs, few telephones, no large PXs, and no indoor flush toilets. In fact, I consider being able to watch an outdoor movie or drink a beer that is truly cold real luxuries. I've had one hot shower and one hot water shave since I've been in Phu Bai. But again, it could be worse.

The pictures of Shannon are great. She is so prissy and mischievous looking. I can't wait to see her reaction to me and whether she will make the connection between pictures and the real me.

I am writing this at 10:00 AM since I am off today. I got to bed at 12:30 after being AOD and then had to get up at 7:30 and get dressed and walk 100 yards in the rain to turn in my report. It has been raining for four days and nights now.

I wanted to call you by MARS (radio phone), but that seems to be worse than long distance. You have to get up early in the morning and place the call and then they call you back, which is usually after noon when they get it through. I am all over the hospital during the day so might be hard to run down. Plus, there are always 6–8 people in the little room where I work and I would hate to have to yell to you in front of an audience."

Sept 21. "Today a skeleton was brought in by an American adviser. The Vietnamese he got it from had dug it up. He was apparently a Marine that could have been separated from his unit, captured and executed by the VC way back in 1966. His family had probably hoped he was a POW all this time. The MPs and Graves Registration came to try to get a clue as to who he was and I'm sure they can, as part of his name was in his boot and his skull still had his teeth."

We interfaced a lot with Graves Registration personnel. They took custody of all bodies in Nam and handled identification of remains, embalming, preserving, and shipping them back to the U.S.

"Most of the officers and enlisted men spent this evening sandbagging the nurses' area. Believe it or not, most of the hooches have never been sandbagged in all these years. There is a rumor that the compound was rocketed sometime in the past and that the NVA commander sent an apology since we treat so many NVA and VC, often not even knowing it. Sounds implausible to me, though. [This turned out to be true. See 1LT Mike Sabo's comments in A Trooper's Story.] I intend to bag my hooch if I can get the material or move to a hooch that is bagged.

Hooray! I finally got the call through. I just wish there was a better way. I waited a while in line to be sure no one cut in. When I finally got you the soldier that was up next kept looking in the booth and could hear everything I said. I hope cassette tapes work out well as the phone situation is not good."

SEPT 22. "I saw my first NVA today. He was brought in by a Major, a Sergeant Major and two other officers, all of them S-2 (Intelligence guys) who clearly wanted us to save their prisoner for interrogation purposes."

This was standard procedure whenever we received enemy patients.

"He had an M16 bullet hole beneath his right eye and it had exited at the top of his head. He was still alive, but not very lively. I watched a doctor use a chrome brace and bit to manually drill into his cranium to relieve pressure. That was a first for me.

I was interested in the reaction of the ER crew to him. They were efficient enough, but in a lively, upbeat mood and didn't seem too worried about whether he lived or died. You can't blame them, though, and I'll bet the NVA doctors are the same way about U.S. prisoners."

I never learned whether he lived or not, but after all these years, I still remember looking down on him with compassion as a human being. He seemed very young, just like our soldiers, but then I wasn't fighting to the death against these guys. My longtime friend, Dr. Mike Sabo, who was a 101st platoon leader and who was critically wounded by the NVA, told me he came to despise them because they frequently raided villages and took girls twelve years and older and made them sex slaves and mules to carry their equipment and supplies until they were used up. Then they were disposed of, just thrown away. Mike said it was terribly upsetting to patrol into a village that had recently been raided and to hear the wails of the families of these girls whom they knew they would never see again.

"Another patient we received today was a Vietnamese civilian who was supposedly an inspector for the secret police in Hue. The civilian hospitals don't want anything to do with people who work with the Americans, especially secret type work. U.S. personnel are not being allowed to enter Hue any more due to anti-American demonstrations. I think a GI shot someone there a week ago and feelings are running pretty strong."

SEPT 23. "I have 5 men who work under me, all E-4s and E-5s. They are good workers and I like them all except one who drives me up the wall. He is a wise guy with a very foul mouth who tries to be the big deal and who is obviously not. I'm going to have a talk with him. I have another who is very sharp and real nice. He has a 6-month-old daughter he has never seen.

I heard from a LTC at supper that we will probably close this hospital right after Christmas. He also said that officers were only getting released if they had less than 60 days until ETS (Estimated Time of Separation) when their hospital closes. That makes it look bad for us.

I heard that mail doesn't come in here for a week at a time during monsoons, so I'd better try to prepare myself for that. I'd better close this so it will get in today's mail. I write so that you will hopefully get a letter every day."

Janie recently (2022) told me she would wait by her parents' front door mail slot when she heard the postman coming and try to grab my letters, before they hit the floor.

SEPT 24. "Well, no mail again today. Maybe I'll get a bunch tomorrow. I ordered and wrote a check for Christmas gifts for my parents today, so you should be getting two canceled checks from PACEX (Pacific Exchange System) in a month or two.

Today we received another unfortunate accident victim. Two pilots were downed in a LOH (OH-6 light observation helicopter also called a LOACH) in the jungle. They were being winched up on a Jungle Penetrator cable by a Huey dustoff when the harness broke. They fell 100 ft back into the jungle. One was killed and we admitted the other with broken arms, legs, pelvis, and ribs. That's a hard way to go after being shot down and to be so close to safety.

I saw a good movie last night called *Fools* with Jason Robarts and Katherine Ross. It was a welcome relief from the depressing shows about race and antiwar demonstrations we've been seeing.

A strange thing happened last week. A colored sergeant was brought in who had a large knot on his head. He claimed he was walking the perimeter of his fire base when someone knocked him out from behind. He said when he came to he had been drugged and that he vaguely remembers being questioned by some "gooks" and that there was one person he thought was Caucasian who spoke English with them. He said he remembered traveling in some kind of vehicle. He was found near a road three days later about 25 miles from where he was abducted. I don't know whatever became of him, but he was taken away by MPs and Military Intelligence. All here who talked to him said he acted like he was on the level, but no one could figure why he was released if it was the VC or NVA who captured him. Weird!

How far does Shannon go by herself and how stable is her walking now? Gosh, I wish I could see her and YOU!"

SEPT 25. "Hooray! I got 4 letters today from you. When the guy walked in with the mail, I felt like I used to before a quiz. I was so psyched up hoping I would get a letter — after only two days without. You express your feelings so well. Maybe we just each understand how the other feels. May our love forever remain as strong as we feel it now.

We had five BCs plus one KIA come in at lunchtime today. They were all from a booby trap. One was an ARVN who wasn't expected to survive his head wound. The worst of the GIs had a third of his jaw blown away and the fragment had gone under his skin and behind his neck and may have done spinal damage. He also had broken arms and leg and was bleeding profusely. He was as good as dead when brought in and in fact a medic was pumping his chest when the dustoff landed. A tracheostomy was performed on him and they got him going again and thought he would make it.

Admissions clerk Spec.4 Bob Randall. Patient belongings were secured in the room on the left. Phu Bai dustoff radio is in the room on the right. Emergency room is immediately to the right.

I was busier than I have been so far regulating medivac choppers to get him and the ARVN down to Da Nang to a neurosurgeon. We have a radio on which we take requests for dustoffs and receive word from incoming ships as to when they will arrive and the nature of the wounds and how many gurneys will be needed. I don't really get involved until the doc says "move 'em out." Usually, we have an EM who specializes in setting up medivacs, but when he is gone, one of two or three of us can do it. We typically ask Da Nang to send a chopper up as we only have one chopper of our own and it must be available in case we get another call.

Warrant Officers Price and O'Conner. They were superb dust-off pilots. Basketball players-not so much.

I am also Communications Officer for the 85th. Last night our radio went out and I really had to do some jumping to get some other unit to monitor our calls until we could get another radio or get ours fixed. Fortunately, we got it all worked out and received no calls. I'm still unsure of my efforts in a lot of areas and I learned a lot in a hurry last night.

We went out to the foothills to fire our weapons today for familiarization. (Under the Geneva Convention, MSCs are the only medical officers allowed to carry automatic weapons.) I had been issued a .45 pistol (1911 model) and was glad for the chance to shoot it. It seemed pretty stiff and a little cantankerous, but I couldn't hit much with it anyway. There was a convoy escort vehicle there that fired, too. It is a big 5-ton beast that has armored plating and is equipped with two .50 cal. and four .30 cal. machine guns. They patrol along the convoys for protection and we see them a lot cruising up and down Highway One, which runs the entire length of Nam and which passes our front gate. I was impressed when those guns opened up on the hillside, never having seen something so small be so destructive. What awesome weapons man has created for his wars!"

SEPT 26. "Today has been slow, but we did get in a few BCs. This time some engineers were clearing a mine field and spotted a mine. They were carefully backing away from it when one of them stepped on a dud artillery round and it exploded. One was killed, one lost his foot and the other two had fragmentation wounds all over their bodies.

Also, today I learned that the GI who was so badly burned by the white phosphorus grenade when I first got here died a few days later. Usually, we don't hear what happens to the patients we evacuate.

To answer a few of your questions, we have a radio station that transmits all over Nam. It plays all the pop music plus a few country and western and some jazz as well as Chicken Man. Actually, it's a better station than most of those in the U.S."

It was called American Forces Vietnam Network (AFVN) and played news on the hour and their Stateside Survey, providing reminders of home. It was played by everyone everywhere and was within earshot as consistently as the sound of choppers. See *Good Morning, Vietnam* with Robin Williams.

"I have electricity to my hooch and have two light bulbs and two small fans. The catalog from which stereo equipment can be ordered is called PACEX. It is a mail order PX in Japan.

This seems like a flat letter, but I feel flat. Must be constipated. I take a malaria pill tomorrow — that will solve that."

SEPT 27. "I've been playing volleyball again today. The weather has been quite nice — not rainy and not too hot and humid. Please send me 2 or 3 pairs of white athletic socks with good elastic. The hooch maids wash clothes every day and that consists of scrubbing them with a brush and pan of soapy water over a piece of steel panel. Then they hang them wherever they can, which is usually on the concertina perimeter wire. Needless to say, clothes are rough and wear out rapidly.

This week we've received a lot of casualties and more deaths than usual. That's real fishy, in that we've seen almost as many U.S. as ARVNs. They fought the supposedly big and successful Lam Son 810 offensive 2 weeks ago in which we (U.S.) were not even offensively engaged. Most of our casualties have been mine and booby trap victims — frequently the result of lack of training or lack of caring on the part of the ARVNs. They seem to be notorious about not mapping their own mine fields and then calling on U.S. engineers to clear them when they want to go back in. Yesterday they brought in one dead, one with his foot blown off, and 3 more with frag wounds all over. The day before it was 2 dead and 3 seriously wounded, one with half his jaw blown away.

The explosion you asked about was demolition of old ammo and explosives (ordnance). They do it every so often and it really shakes up the whole place. There is an ARVN base camp and boot camp just down the road and they seem to fire off explosions and small arms at will. These little people are really something. They make sharp looking soldiers, but I wonder how good they can be. GIs seem to be 50% tougher with 100% more will to live. The ARVNs seem ready to give up the ghost with wounds that would hardly slow GIs. I've seen the docs just shake their head when an ARVN would die and a GI with similar wounds would pull through.

It amazes me when a GI comes in with an arm and leg blown off (traumatic amputation) and still be conscious and able to give us his name and unit and next of kin. It's sad because the victims of explosive blasts have very great tendencies to come in missing one or two extremities, yet alert with a seemingly good chance of pulling through. Then about 12 to 24 hours later they die from respiratory failure. A doc told me it is thought that the shock waves from the blast cause some sort of deterioration in the vascular system that progresses to the lungs with time and they become unable to transfer gases with the blood."

This malady was called Shock Lung in Nam, and later became known as Adult or Acute Respiratory Distress Syndrome. When I got home and was in graduate school, I was hired by Upjohn Pharmaceuticals for a sales position from among hundreds of applicants at SFASU. Turns out Upjohn was researching the possible benefits of its drug Solu-Medrol in treating ARDS. Maybe I was hired because I was their only applicant who was conversant about the syndrome.

LETTER TO PARENTS: "No, I have no plans and couldn't wander off and go fishing if I wanted to. Each unit area is separated by concertina wire and guard posts and then all those are fenced in by the base perimeter which is fenced, mined, and guarded. The base is surrounded by electronic sensors that set off alarms when approached. There are also ambushes set up at night and flares are set off all night long. The hospital is on the edge of the base perimeter and therefore is probably its weakest point.

Dustoff is a chopper that picks up the injured. They swoop down and are gone again typically in a tremendous cloud of dust. They have red crosses on them and are not armed, as opposed to the slicks. Slicks are the same type chopper (UH-1 or Huey) only they frequently have M60 machine guns mounted in each side door. We often have patients brought in by slicks. When we evacuate an urgent case to the 95th Evac in Da Nang, it is usually by a dustoff. Occasionally, it is by Chinook (CH-47) if a lot of equipment is required to life-support the patient."

C-130s, also called the Hercules, which are large, four-engine turbo propped airplanes, were frequently used to evac, too. They were all over Vietnam and are still in use today. I asked Rex Keese, a friend and former USAF "Herk" pilot whether I was right about the engines because they landed and took off very efficiently on our short runway.

His response was, "That's exactly right. Allison T-56 engines with Hamilton Standard props. Early on in Nam, the Herk A models had three-bladed props. All later models were four-bladed. The 'Four Fans of Freedom' was the 'Queen of the Skies' and 'The Workhorse of the Nation!' Amen and Amen. Every Herk driver on the planet will tell you the same thing!"

Those C-130 Herk evacuations were considerably more complicated in that we were interfacing with the Air Force, which had its own regulations and ways of doing things. They were much more strict about following procedures than we were on helicopter evacs, but then, patients for which C-130s were required were usually extremely critical and were being flown to distant and better-equipped hospitals. They were staffed with critical care specialists, whereas dustoffs carried a medic.

SEPT 28. "We had to admit one of our clerks today. He is an addict and was violently opposed to being admitted, but he has been passing out over his typewriter and vomiting every hour. Our Registrar, Bill Green, for whom he clerked, admitted him for his own good. It was just a matter of time before he overdoses. He is 19, and just got back from 40 days AWOL in the U.S. where he got married. That's a simplified explanation, but I think that's how he explained it.

Also, he has spent time in Ft. Leavenworth prison. He has also been detoxified twice before on the amnesty program, so his life is really worth little in terms of time remaining, I would say. It's hard to understand how these guys keep getting hooked when they can see their friends turning into purposeless beings so often.

We received a First Sergeant early this morning who had been fragged at about 4:00 AM. Someone rolled a grenade under his bunk (or possibly under his floor) and blew away most of his buttocks and mangled his legs, but it looks as though he will pull through with no loss of limb or life. He was extremely lucky. I'm just thankful I'm not in a command position."

It made me a little nervous that my hooch mate was CO of our enlisted men. So many of them were on heroin and he was judge and jury on most infractions, frequently administering Article 15s that could affect passes, leave, pay, jail time, etc. He was always distant and seemed nervous, and I don't blame him.

SEPT 29. "I am now spending most of my time in the Registrar Office, away from the ER and it seems very slow. A lot of the registrar function is keeping records and statistics and it is hard to get interested when someone is telling about adding columns of numbers and typing them in little squares. I'm sure time will go faster when I become the registrar and assume all that responsibility. That may not happen though, as two hospitals to the south are closing and their registrars will have to go somewhere. Bill Green leaves in December.

We have really seen a lot of casualties the last two days, 5 dead and 8–10 wounded. We had been averaging about 3 WIAs (Wounded in Action) the days before. I was told that they are a result of the pull out. As our patrols decrease, the VC and NVA fall in behind us and plant lots of booby traps and that's what most of our casualties have been a result of. That seems a terrible way to get it. At least if you're shooting at the enemy, you would have the satisfaction of knowing you might hurt him, too. Also, the mortality rate from GSWs is much less than from fragmentation weapons."

SEPT 30. "Today I ordered a Yashica Electro 35 GS camera with wide angle and telephoto lenses. $50. Please send me some 35mm color film, as its next to impossible to buy any in Phu Bai.

Yesterday one of our convoys got hit by a rocket and mortar attack going to Da Nang. Rockets hit in front and behind a truck driven by one of our hospital sergeants, but no one was hurt. The infamous Hải Vân Pass they were going through was in the clouds and they couldn't get air support and couldn't see anything. The convoy escorts (that I described Sept. 25) opened up and the VC stopped shooting. Now I'm sure I won't be driving to Da Nang. I flew through the pass on my way to Phu Bai and it gave me the creeps from way above. It is so vulnerable and such a perfect ambush spot when it is too thick to fly.

Hope Shannon is still off her pacifier. I wish I could give her a big squeeze right now. I just ache for you both."

A 101st Trooper's Story

Of all the booby trap victims we saw, I never got to interview any of them as to how their incident happened and was curious what that looked like, especially the actions of the medical and dustoff personnel that were involved.

My friend Dr. Michael J. Sabo was a 101st 1st Lt. and had been wounded and medivaced to the 85th a few months before I got there. I called him in November 2022 to learn more. This is part of what he shared:

"In early 1971, the 101st Airborne Division participated in Operation Lam Son 719, the invasion of Laos bordering I Corps, the northernmost region of South Vietnam.

As platoon leader/pathfinder for 3rd platoon, Delta Company, 1/502 battalion, my mission was to air assault by Huey into the Ruong Ruong Valley (the "valley of death") to pursue and engage a battalion of about 200 NVA sappers.

We had to aggressively pursue and push the NVA, knowing they would be setting traps to slow us down. Their favorite was a grenade with shortened fuse for immediate explosion when the spoon (handle) is released.

The floor of this triple canopy jungle is a mat of rotting vegetation and vines which sinks as it is stepped on. The grenade is placed in the vegetation at the side of the trail and the spoon is tied to a ground vine, then barely placed in the retaining hole so only a slight step on the vine pulls out the pin. Immediate explosion, no delay results. These types of grenades have a fifteen-foot lethal radius.

As we cleared another ridge line, the triple canopy was about 100 feet high and the undergrowth lessened except for a heavy mat of ground vines. I was walking eight to ten meters behind point with my rifle at the ready. The vegetative mat had a lot of give with each step, depressing the ground vines.

Suddenly, an extremely loud explosion erupted to my right rear, approximately 8 feet from me, well within the lethal zone. (Troopers behind me later told how close it was and that they thought I was dead.) The force of the explosion threw me upwards and to the left, my right ear deafened, body shook like a giant had grabbed me and shook me. Every part of me shuddered, and the pain was extremely severe. I burned on the inside and outside. I had never felt pain as bad then or since.

Abruptly, I hit the ground face down. The right side of my head and ear were burning and felt gone. Right elbow was hit, right wrist into hand, thumb was hit with flexor tendons exposed at the wrist, and the base of the thumb muscles torn from wrist to thumb. Right flank and torso had multiple hits, one stuck in the muscle over the right kidney. The left leg calf muscle was shredded and bleeding profusely. My troopers noted later that the wounds were smoking as well as my fatigues.

Our medic, Doc, was way back in the line and somehow was hit in the upper-left chest. He did not hesitate, ran forward, patched up Lee who had been lightly peppered and then came to me. In the meantime, I ordered my radio operator to order Cobra gunships to our position. Doc got to me and kept me from bleeding out while he was bleeding from the chest. He refused to treat or even pressure bandage himself until Lee and I were stable. I wrote him up for the Silver Star while in the 85th Evac Hospital at Phu Bai.

We were so far out, close to the A Shau Valley and Laos that the medevac choppers took 45 minutes to reach us. My men cleared a small area of saplings and bushes, but the 100-foot-tall canopy required a jungle penetrator to be lowered by cable and it could not reach the jungle floor. It must touch the ground to discharge static electricity. The pilots were so good, they lowered the Huey into the treetops and chopped the top branches enough to lower in among the trees without hitting large limbs which would crash the chopper.

When they did this, I had been laid on my back in the small clearing, the limbs and debris came down on us, and we thought the chopper was crashing down on us. Two of my young troopers threw themselves across me to take the crashing chopper in their backs, great men at the age of nineteen. Fortunately, the pilots were expert, did not crash, and winched up Doc, Lee, and me as two Cobras mini-gunned and rocketed all around us. We flew to Phu Bai and the 85th Evac Hospital.

Two E-5 medics opened me up while waiting for the surgeon. Another three troopers were brought in at the same time from another unit. The general surgeon then arrived, had us all in a circle in the OR, and worked on all of us with no anesthesia except a rubber bar in our teeth and large straps on metal tables. He opened my left leg deeply to the back of the tibia (lower leg bone) while removing muscle. I watched his hand enter deeply and when the instrument hit bone, I told him where he was. He continued. I spit out the rubber bar in my teeth and said, "I thought this went out in the Civil War." He apologized and stated he had to stop the bleeding, but could not remove the metal, so he may have to remove my left leg at the knee. I asked him to do whatever else he could, but keep the leg on.

He then removed more muscle and packed a large amount of Nu Gauze in the leg to slow the bleeding. He also packed and probed my right wrist to thumb. The straps held. Later, I realized that if I had the benefit of anesthesia and was unconscious, the leg might have been removed. He did tell me there was no time for anesthesia if it had been available anyway. If he waited, I would bleed out. They then put the rubber bar back into my mouth.

When they wheeled me out, I noticed two medics with mops soaking up my blood from under and around the surgical table—apparently a significant amount of blood. The surgeon kept all six of us alive and all our limbs on.

Three days later, we talked, and he told me he had been drafted out of his general surgery residency before his final year. I felt sorry for him since he was doing all the specialties—general, orthopedics, vascular, neuro. All OJT (on-the-job training).

Nine days at 85th Evac and then medevaced to the naval hospital ship, *Sanctuary* for one month (reworked wounds and removed three more pieces of metal and pants material from left leg)."

Inspired by his own medical experiences, after his discharge Sabo went on to become a podiatrist, was board certified in both foot and ankle surgery, and practiced for thirty-two years in Lufkin, Texas, where he and I became friends. In our discussions of his treatment at the 85th, I mentioned that I had heard the hospital had endured a rocket attack some time back, and that the NVA commander had sent an apology, apparently because we had treated enemy troops over the years. I had dismissed this as a rumor, which was normal in Nam since no one had memories further back than their own one year (or less) time served (our personal time snapshot). However, Mike stunned me when he told me he was there during the attack. Following is his account:

"I have bragged on Army and Navy nurses for the last fifty-one years as the "bravest of the brave." My first night in the 85th Evac hospital, Phu Bai, the compound was hit with 122mm rockets by the NVA. Fortunately, they missed the buildings and no deaths occurred. This was on 12 March 1971. Most of us could not move out of bed due to being positioned in place, myself positioned on my left side with pillows packed to my lower back, left leg elevated, and right arm elevated, wrapped. The nurses were young, recently out of training and all had volunteered for combat-zone assignment. They were all under "standing orders" to go directly to the bunkers whether on or off duty if the hospital was attacked. ALL NURSES came to the wards, none to the bunkers, turned on low lights and came to our sides with hands on us to reassure us that we were secure and safe. They defied the rules to care for their patients and placed themselves in mortal danger. I love them. Whenever I meet a military nurse, she gets a hug and an explanation. They are always with me."

A follow-up comment I would add to Mike's story: We, and I suspect most, military hospitals were staffed primarily with young physicians who learned to perform well beyond their training. They just had to do whatever it took in many situations to save life or limb. Those who I talked to later all thought they were better doctors for their experiences in Vietnam. In fact, our whole team learned by OJT most days. I don't see how young men and women who are under two or three-year commitments could ever be trained to handle all the situations that war throws at them.

October 1971

OCT 2. "I got your tape yesterday. It was great to hear all of you and especially you and Shannon. Our daughter is so smart! It really gave me a thrill to hear her and I laughed at her duck and cow and the monkey and the big "light!" I hope to begin a tape soon, but want to see what else is in the package you sent. I hate to tape over my only voice contact with you and Shannon.

We, as well as all of VN, are under yellow alert until Oct 4 due to the national elections. That means all groups must disperse by 10:00 p.m. and flak jackets and helmets must be kept within reach at all times. An awful lot of artillery and mortars have been fired from Phu Bai the last two nights—the close ones have woken me up a couple of times. That is indeed a strange feeling to jump straight up and wonder what woke you and to try to decide whether you need to run for a bunker while you're more asleep than awake. Fortunately, it's all been outgoing so far.

I worked late tonight and about 7:00 p.m. a captain brought in 17 men that needed rabies shots. They had all been bitten, scratched, or licked by a puppy that died of rabies today. It is very prevalent here, in fact, one of my sergeants is presently undergoing the shots. He was bitten by a rat as he slept. Rats, dogs, and roaches are almost out of control. I keep no food in my hooch, and it's too tight for rats to get in, and I don't pet any dogs, so maybe I will be safe from that end of it.

I hope to start taping some of the sounds of our world over here. I think it would be interesting to record a dustoff radio conversation, an ER when several casualties come in, or outgoing artillery, but no incoming, hopefully. Also, I hope you get recordings of Shannon's vocabulary to keep over the years."

If I made those Vietnam sound recordings, we have never found them.

"Today marked my first month in Nam. Sometimes (seldom) I feel as though time is going fast, but then I think of what I have left and it slows to a crawl."

OCT 4. "I would so like to see Shannon. Hope she is still pottying. I thought of her so much this evening. Honey, of all the horribly sad things I've seen here, only tonight did I have to fight back tears. A little Vietnamese baby, the same size as Shannon was brought in by her mother. She wasn't breathing and the staff worked frantically on her for 15 minutes until we learned from the interpreter that she had been found floating face down in a ditch and had been missing for 30 minutes before being found. The doctors finally gave up then. It was so sad to see that chubby baby lying there lifeless and staring at the ceiling. Seeing that poor mother thank us all and wrap her baby in a blanket and walk out with tears streaming down her face just broke my heart. I didn't tell you this to sadden you, Darling, as I know it would, but only to share with you something that touched me so deeply, and to remind ourselves how closely we must watch our little bundle of joy.

I hate to end a letter on such a note, but I have trouble thinking much past that, except for how deeply I love my girls and how I long for you both. I would do anything to have you in my arms right now. Only 6 months and 24 days left to go!

P.S. We are evacing a GI tomorrow to the U.S. to have 4 of his toes amputated. He's only been here 2 weeks, but he has 14 toes. We all got a laugh from that."

OCT 5. "The weather reports say we are to be hit by a typhoon within the next 24 hours. Don't know yet what all that entails, but it's not hard to guess since it is the equivalent of a hurricane. I sure hope we miss it, as this little plywood shack I live in ain't my idea of a storm shelter.

I put in for R&R for January 3rd today, but I will have to be very lucky to get it, as priority is given to the ones who have been in-country longest, regardless of rank. February will be more likely. Hong Kong is no longer an R&R site and Australia won't be after Dec. 1, so more pressure will be put on Hawaii.

I played basketball tonight and it really did me in. We have an old French hangar next to our compound that has been converted into a gym. The exercise always makes me feel better. Maybe if I keep it up, I'll break a leg and get sent home.

My boss, an MSC Major, is pretty cantankerous and seems to raise hell frequently and he doesn't like me. I am with the majority, though, when I say I am not particularly fond of him either. Bill Green (who the XO likes even less) and I laugh him off as much as possible. Enough of that."

I can't remember his name, but he was Regular Army (career) and boasted he had only been with his family about a year out of the previous three, due to volunteering or being selected for various deployments.

OCT 6. "I got all sweaty playing basketball and then nearly froze when I showered. We do have a small water heater, but there is seldom any hot water due to all the people using it. I've gotten 2 or 3 warm showers from it. Still haven't seen the typhoon, so hoping we won't get hit.

We never saw any violence during the elections. We are down the road a piece from the village of Phu Bai, although

Letters Home from 85th Evacuation Hospital Vietnam, 1971

I don't think it was hit either. I've decided the reason all the combat units are based here is because of the airport. It is called the Hue-Phu Bai Airport and has been here for years."

Actually, the airport can still be seen if googled, and apparently, it is now a regional airport for that area. Look for Phu Bai or Huong Thuy on Google Earth. There are no remnants of the 85th that I can see.

"The only interesting thing I did today was watch a spinal tap performed on a guy who had been having blackouts. We scrunched him up in a fetal position on his side and held him tight while the Dr. stuck a 6-inch needle in his spine and then took samples of the fluid that dripped out and measured the fluid pressure. I watch everything I can and find it all very interesting, although sometimes I get a little tight in the stomach. One of the anesthetists invited me to watch surgery since he had seen me hanging around the ER and pre-op so much. I have also asked the X-Ray people to teach me to take X-Rays since they get in a bind sometimes and I often feel useless when casualties come in. My main purpose in A&D is to oversee what goes on and be sure that the radio is covered at all times, and that is not difficult at all, so I have the time right now.

I've wondered a few times whether I shouldn't consider med school when I get out, but I don't want anything that will take away from you girls. If I only knew what I was going to do when I get out, it would sure take a load off. I know we both are going to want so much to have a place of our own as soon as possible.

One of our men was found hanging by his belt from the ceiling this morning. He lived, and we sent him down to a psychiatrist in Da Nang, all sedated and strapped to a litter. It's really not hard to see how a weak or troubled person could turn to drugs or suicide in this country. I see so very little of the hardships many of them face and have so few of their problems, yet I know how I long to escape and how frustrated I get at times myself (but certainly not to any extreme). I do know how much I depend on your strength and love and letters, and I can just imagine what a "Dear John" letter would do to a person over here. What an emotional bomb that would be! I really have to appreciate Dear Abby for her standing advice to girls to wait 'til the guy returns to tell him.

P.S. This is the province of Thua Thien, and the next province just a few miles north of us is Quảng Tri. It borders the DMZ; in case you see us in the papers. Actually, it seems as if most of the action is now in the south. The further the better. I'll keep my fingers crossed."

OCT 7. "I am AOD tonight and have 5 hours to go before I can go to bed. This really is going to get old, as I pull it every 5 to 7 days and must stay up at least until 12:30 and then go to work at the usual time of 7:30. And to make matters worse, Bill Green leaves tomorrow for 10 days' leave in Australia. That leaves me holding a big bag.

We have two major inspections coming up in the next two months, and now that I know I'm getting out, it's difficult to put forth the effort and do my best. Everyone knows they will be here for only a few more months and therefore have lax attitudes. And when they really get short (on time remaining), they can become pretty worthless. Bill and I are recommending the Army Commendation Medal be withdrawn from a Sgt. that leaves in two weeks, as well as removing his name from the E-6 promotion list. He works for me in A&D and has become very belligerent. He went to Da Nang today without authority plus got drunk last night and left his job, so I am fed up. It's kind of hard though to get worked up over some things, since I don't like being here any better than anyone else.

I'm glad you have Shannon to comfort you, as well as your family. How are things going at home? Are all of Shannon's teeth in now? I hope all your problems there are tiny."

OCT 10. "It is Sunday night, raining, no mail, and I just listened to Texas get stomped by OU. And I miss you.

I ran into a guy today I had known at Ft. Sam. He is a pilot and has been here 16 months straight because he loves flying so much. To each his own!"

In retrospect, I can understand that many men liked being in Nam, especially if they had major issues in their lives back "in the world." I guess all wars have the attractions of interesting sights, sounds, adventure, danger, excitement, and weirdness. It is unique in the human experience.

"We had a hi-bye (hello newbies, goodbye oldies) party at our officers' club tonight that had really good food. I ate 8 oz. of ground round, an 8 oz. sirloin, and about a dozen boiled shrimp, not to mention baked potato, beans, rolls, cake, and beer. It was fantastic and a welcome change from mess hall food, which honestly is pretty good, although whatever is left over usually gets served in some form the next day.

I got a call from an MSC captain (Burt Wilde) down at the 91st Evac at Chu Lai who will be coming here next month when they close down. He has experience in the registrar field, so I'm glad to be getting someone who knows, hopefully, more than I do. I suppose I will still become the registrar though, as I am senior in grade to him.

We got another NVA in tonight. He has multiple frag wounds over his body and both feet were blown off, so he may not live. I'll try to remember to tell you more about the POWs and defectors we get in on my next tape. It's a long story and my wrist is getting tired as I just finished a letter to my folks."

I don't remember if I ever wrote about or recorded that information, but so far have not come across anything in my records.

Letters Home from 85th Evacuation Hospital Vietnam, 1971

OCT 11. "I have a cold now and don't feel like doing anything. It's been raining non-stop for two days and I hope it doesn't rain tomorrow night when I have AOD. Also, I hear another typhoon is headed this way. Ugh!

Another tragic thing happened last night. One of the dustoff choppers went down near here. It belonged to Eagle Dustoff, the medivac company stationed at Camp Eagle, about 5 miles north of us. They bring most of the patients from the 101st to us. All 4 crew members died, as it crashed into a bay. What makes it so sad is that the patient they were picking up was already dead or died shortly after the crash. And if that were not enough, the guy was playing Russian roulette with himself so probably didn't care if he lived or not. Things like that are what frustrates me so much. There are just so many ways to get screwed up in this godforsaken place that getting hurt by the enemy seems to be a lesser concern. It was pitch black and raining last night and the pilots usually won't fly in weather like that. I only know a couple of pilots from Eagle, but don't know if they were victims, yet. Incidentally, our radio was out at the time all this happened and I was tearing around trying to get us back in operation, although I doubt our radio working would have made any difference. We might have heard their last transmission, however.

Tonight, I was called from the mess hall for an "emergency call" from Saigon that scared me to death. I thought something had happened to one of you girls, but it was the USO trying to connect a patient's wife with me. We had reported her husband as seriously ill (encephalitis), and for some reason his wife wanted to talk to the registrar. I went and found the doctor that was treating the guy and told him to call her back. I'm not allowed to give out any information, naturally.

We had a patient scheduled to be sent back to the states today for hepatitis, but he disappeared. He has a history of drug abuse, so I imagine he just had to have another hit, or didn't want to leave all this cheap heroin. That is quite typical of these tortured souls."

OCT 12. "I got two letters from you today (Oct. 5 & 7) and that cheered me up. Isn't it something that just those pieces of paper can mean so much to a person?

I enjoy the pictures of our photogenic little girl so very much, and you both look just great. I'm glad you send a few at a time. I look at them over and over all day.

I've learned that the Army is releasing people from Nam up to six months early for school at its own discretion. The main problem is that they request 4 months' notice. I was previously accepted at SFA and Texas A&I, but by the time all the paperwork was assembled, I doubt I'd have time to get it in before the semester started. I just read today that all junior officers are being released up to 4 months early, except for JAG, MSC, physicians, dentists, etc. That hurts."

OCT 13. "I had planned to call you in Lufkin tonight, but when I checked with the MARS station, they said reception was poor due to the monsoons, and if I got a call through at all, it might be 3 or 4:00 a.m. here. The MARS calls are radio relayed so that the cost of the call is based only on the distance from the station in the U.S. to Texas. Usually, the calls are picked up in California, so we only pay long-distance rates from there to Houston. Regular long-distance calls from here are computed at $3.60/minute. If I can move into Bill Green's hooch in December, I will be able to call MARS easily, since he has a phone. As it is now, I would end up calling from my office, which is always full of people.

Today I was sitting in the chow hall talking football with a doctor friend from Alabama (Bill Harmon), and a doctor named Charlie Railsback with whom I've become acquainted asked if I was from Texas. Turns out he went to [Texas] Tech and was in Ken's class in medical school. [Ken is Janie's brother and was a USAF Flight Surgeon serving in California at that time. He later became an orthopedic surgeon in Houston.] Naturally, he knew Ken and Hog and all their friends. I was delighted to find someone from Texas, at last, much less someone who knew my own relatives. I think that he is very short here, though." [His time left in Nam was short.]

OCT 14. "We had a show at the club tonight that was really good (Korean performers). They played a lot of neat songs, including "The Eyes of Texas." I wish I had taken a tape recorder because the response of the audience was really fun. Any time we have a show, we are flooded by pilots and they take the place over. They sound like Aggies with their chants and yells, but when you remember these guys lay it on the line day after day and then see them come in all up, you can appreciate their esprit and actually yell with them. I'm beginning to understand the reactions of the GIs to the Bob Hope shows now. Just anything at all that hints of home is welcomed tremendously and the bands, usually Filipino or Korean, always play U.S. songs, and especially country and western. Everyone loves it.

OCT 15. "For some reason, we have suddenly been receiving a lot of battle casualties, most of them very bad, with a lot of traumatic amputations. I think of the last twelve, three have been 1ˢᵗLts. At 7:00 a.m. today I was going to breakfast when a dustoff landed with one, a terrible way to start one's day. This Lt. had his leg blown almost off at the hip, plus chunks of his other one, as well as his right hand. I won't describe the details, but I will say seeing these horrors leave a feeling in me that defies description and leaves me subdued for the rest of the day. We always go through the wallets of the wounded to learn all we can of them as well as to secure their valuables. This Lt. was a 1970 graduate of West Point. He had a family portrait with him in his cadet uniform, his two younger brothers and parents, all with such proud looks on their faces. I guess it was that picture that made this case get to me worse than most.

Letters Home from 85th Evacuation Hospital Vietnam, 1971

Yesterday we got another Lt. with both his legs gone, plus an EM (enlisted man) with one gone and the other mangled. I find it hard to understand how a man can force himself to keep going out, knowing that something like that could happen to him. If they saw much of these injuries, I don't think they could. I know I couldn't.

Today the company commander of the Lt. missing both legs came in to find out how much his wife had been told of his injuries. The Lt. was planning to call his wife tonight, and the CO wanted to be sure he wouldn't have to be the one to tell her he had lost both of his legs. Can you imagine the nightmare that would be? When we call in to the USARV (U.S. Army Republic of Vietnam) headquarters in Long Binh (they relay info to the U.S.), we always are required to give the most complete diagnosis and prognosis possible. I'm sure it's best that the next of kin know as much as possible to preclude something like the above from happening.

Also, last night, a dead guy was brought in that had apparently been shot as he slept by someone on the patrol with him. An autopsy was requested on him and a big investigation is starting about that.

Don't feel bad if you sounded depressed in places on your tape because I know I do, too. I don't see any real reason for us to put up fronts to each other. The same goes for the personal part of the tape. But I see no reason why we shouldn't say those things. We are, after all, husband and wife, and those things are strictly between us. We've said and done them with each other, and they were wonderful then, and for that reason I think they still mean a lot, or should, to us. It's just that they were and will be beautiful times again, and the thought of them helps blot out some of the vision of the present. I hope this all makes sense, Darling, for I feel it is very important for us to put our personal thoughts in the open. I think that will become more important as time passes, for as you said, it's the personal parts of the letters and tapes that mean so very much, no matter how interesting the other stuff might be."

OCT 16. "Your letter of the 9th was not post marked in Houston until the 12th. I noticed on another letter also that there was a 3-day delay in post marking.

I don't know if it was just a rumor started over here or if it was true (which I doubt very much), but everyone has been saying that it was predicted by Jean Dixon that Phu Bai would be overrun on Oct 15. Everyone here laughed it off and said Phu Bai looked like it had already been run over. Well, at midnight I was suddenly awakened by artillery and I sat up in a start thinking "Is this it?" We all had a good laugh about it today, since several people thought the same thing. Some of the new folks even ran to bunkers. I've gotten to where I can tell the outgoing almost immediately, and fortunately still haven't heard incoming. The firing went on most of the night, so I recorded some of it just to see what it would sound like on my cassettes. I won't send it, though."

I have yet to find that tape after all these years.

"Tell Shannon for me she is not to tee-tee in or on her birthday presents! That was hilarious. I so wish I could see her. It just kills me to think about that part of her life I'm missing.

Hopefully, we may have a movie tonight. It's been a week since we've had a working projector. *Bob and Carol and Ted and Alice, Tora,* and *Oliver* were sent here, but our projector was busted, so we missed them all."

OCT 17. "Today is Sunday and my day off, but I was awakened at 8:30 because our radio was out again. I got busy and never did get to go back to bed. While we were trying to get radio coverage, a body was brought in that proved to be the result of another tragedy. He was coming in from guard duty last night, and since the enemy had been seen in the area, that caused jumpiness. He was shot by a trigger-happy buddy. Since I've been here, I don't think I've seen a single GI killed by gunfire that wasn't from his own unit. All those killed by enemy have been booby traps and mines. I'll be so glad to get away from all this.

Remember I wrote about the company commander of the Lt. who had lost both legs and how he wanted to be sure the Lieutenant's family knew of his injuries before he called home? Well, today we got a call from the Red Cross about it. He had called his mother and told her he was wounded. The connection was so bad that the family wasn't even sure it was him and they had not been informed by the Army, so they were in a state of panic. I called USARV Casualty Branch in Long Binh and learned that the Dept. of the Army in Washington had not received the teletype that was sent. How terribly sad for such a thing to happen. I'm just glad our end had nothing to do with it getting screwed up."

OCT 18. "I got your letter of the 12th today and you sound so depressed, and I don't blame you. I guess it's hard for me to fully realize what you're going through and vice versa. Nixon is supposed to make some policy change today that a lot over here will hinge on. Hopefully, I may get an early out or something from it—anything to get home and get my precious family back together. I got this info from a 2-star general who toured the hospital yesterday.

I got a long letter from David [my brother] today. It was so terribly sad, and I truly feel sorry for him. I'm sure you must be in the middle of it, and I'm sorry for that. There seems to be so much sadness all around us. I feel it is beating me down, especially on the days when I see mangled and bleeding kids that are that way needlessly.

I don't think it has changed me at all, and no, I'm not tempted by drugs or booze. In fact, I'm on the Drug and Alcohol Dependency Intervention Council of the hospital.

I also got a letter from Gary Mills today in which he told about a friend we went through Basic with who was forced to resign his commission. He served a year over here and then told the Army to get screwed and refused to cut his hair. He was one of the leaders of the "VN Veterans Against the War" march in Washington, D.C. last spring. He has written a book called *Less than Honorable Conditions* about his Army experiences. He is very bright and vibrant. He is presently a hippy and plans to enter politics."

OCT 20. "Today I was going over our evac manifest for the flight tomorrow (C-130 to fly in to pick up patients) and came across a guy from Lufkin. I immediately went to his ward and got acquainted with him. I didn't know him as he was only 21, but he promised to get in touch with my parents when he gets home. He had an appendectomy, and it got infected. He's doing well now, but he's been here for 9 months, so he's being sent home. The doctors here hate the war and the Army, and their motto seems to be "evacuate our fighting strength." I wonder if the Army isn't deliberately looking the other way because every broken bone, malaria, hepatitis, and a large assortment of odds and ends are now tickets home from the 85th.

I'm presently reading *The Great Escape* and like it a lot, maybe because I'd kind of like to tunnel out of here sometimes. I hope to read *The Exorcist* and *The Pentagon Papers* next. I hear they're excellent reads."

OCT 23. "As I write this I am at the office and we are in the midst of Typhoon Hester—quite an experience! Winds are expected to go above 100 mph later today. I don't know how high they are now, but I can see pieces of tin flying off roofs, and no one is allowed to go outside unless it is an emergency, and they must be wearing a helmet. And me with a slight case of diarrhea! It's getting pretty scary, as the wind is roaring in a high moan now, and even inside the building we must yell to communicate. The storm is progressing down the coast. We've learned that power is out at the 95th in Da Nang and that patients are being evacuated from the 91st at Chu Lai, on down the coast from Da Nang. How they are doing it, I don't know because nothing can fly. We heard that the registrar's office and officers' club at the 91st have been blown into the sea (the hospital is on a bluff over the ocean). This place is not nearly so sturdy as the 91st or 95th, so here's hoping the storm blows itself out some before the worst hits. Our dustoff chopper is tied down and has trucks parked all around it to prevent it from blowing over. And to top it all off, I got stuck with AOD tonight because the guy who was scheduled is stranded in Da Nang."

Following is an article I googled in 2022 from *The New York Times* on October 25, 1971:

"Typhoon Hester killed 36 persons, including three Americans in South Vietnam's five northernmost provinces over the weekend, left tens of thousands homeless and badly damaged several American combat bases. The typhoon, with winds of up to 138 mph destroyed the town of Namhoa in Thua Thien Province, 400 miles northeast of Saigon. [That's the province the 85th was in.] Thousands of fishing boats were damaged, and up to 90% of the crops were destroyed. There were no reported combat incidents involving American ground troops today. But U.S. B-52 bombers were reported continuing their pounding of enemy supply lines in southern Laos and Cambodia."

"Our office roof is now leaking pretty badly. I surely hope my hooch is holding up. It was leaking some when I left it 3 hours ago. It's possible to stay pretty dry with the rain gear we're issued, but you sweat a lot wearing it. We are issued rubber overalls, a rubber parka, galoshes, and a poncho.

When Bill Green leaves, I hope to get his hooch. It is closer to the shower and is among all the other hooches. I don't like sitting out in the open and I don't know why our hooch is so far from the others."

OCT 24. "The storm is now past—it slowed down about 10:00 p.m. last night—and no one was hurt. My hooch seems to have gotten the worst of it, as about half the roof got blown off. Someone saw it right after it happened, and my hooch mate, George Bodie, got some men to help him put canvas and sandbags over it so our stuff didn't get very wet at all. Most of the damage was to his half, so he was a little worse off. I had to stay in the HQ to coordinate calls, so didn't get involved with the roof last night.

The storm died down and I got to bed after 1:00 a.m. and got up at 7:00 to start putting the roof back on. It was nice this morning but clouded up after lunch and is now raining again. We put all the tin back on and then tied sandbags all over it to keep it from blowing up in the next storm, which I'm sure will be soon."

Four to six sandbags would be tied along a long wire, then drug over the roof crest like saddlebags. We put so much weight on our roof to secure the tin that the hooch began to tilt and sink into the ground, as I recall.

"None of the buildings got flattened except for a lot of the outhouses, but about one-third of the roof on the hangar (supply and gym) got blown away, and there was minor roof damage to most of the hooches and some of the wards. We consider ourselves very fortunate, for if the storm had hit us as hard as it did Chu Lai, it could have been disastrous since our buildings are temporary structures. I haven't heard how strong the winds got, but I suspect at least 80 mph.

I had to go out in it several times as AOD and that really wore me out. I wore my rain suit and galoshes and pistol, plus my flak jacket and steel helmet as protection against flying debris. That amounts to about 25 lbs. extra weight, and the wind was so strong that just walking was a struggle, so I was exhausted at night's end. It was impossible to face into it, as the rain stung severely, and I wondered if it could cause eye damage. Naturally, there was no electricity anywhere except emergency lighting in the hospital.

The Air Force canceled all our evacs today because all available planes are being used to evac patients from the 91st at Chu Lai. It was decided to go ahead and close it down early since it was so badly damaged. The radio (AFVN) said that only two GIs were killed by the storm, but I doubt that that includes the one we received this afternoon. He was hit in the head by a falling tree. We also treated about 30 GIs for various storm related injuries."

I wrote to my parents on October 29 that we were still on rationed water. Also, the storm had its funny sides, too. We had a good laugh about the outhouse getting blown over with the two guys sitting in it, and the old mangy mutt that let out a surprised yelp when the wind flipped him and blew him down the road a way.

"Enough of the storm. I just hope I never have to ride out another. What a godforsaken country this is with its wars, diseases, storms, heat, floods, insects, and snakes! We had a snake bite case brought in during the storm. A guy was wading a stream, and a snake went up his pant leg. It was apparently nonpoisonous, but can you imagine having a snake bite you under your pants in the dark while fighting a hurricane?"

OCT 25. "We were in our first basketball game tonight since *Hester* when I got called back to A&D to phone in some deaths to USARV Casualty Branch in Long Binh. I must be getting calloused to this war, as these were about as bad as I've seen, and I didn't seem to be particularly phased at the sight, only the smell. The remains were of a Capt. and a 1st Lt. that had crashed in a Cobra several days ago, and naturally they were torn up and infested by maggots. Forgive me for mentioning this. We all speak of death and mutilation as a common occurrence."

OCT 26. "I called my parents today—hope you are not jealous. Just wanted to say hello to them and let you all know the storm had not bested us.

Tonight, at chow, one of the surgeons showed us a clipping his wife has sent him about the West Point Lt. I wrote you about. It showed a picture of him in his cadet uniform. It made us all angry because his dad was an assistant coach at Indiana U and a former star of the 1940s, and the entire article described how great his father had been and barely made mention of the fact that his son had "died of his wounds" in Vietnam. I had never realized how nondescriptive, and for that reason maybe merciful, the word "wounds" is. I must have always thought of wounds as a few clean holes and a little blood just like in the movies."

Shame on those Americans who disrespected our guys who endured so much in a war we didn't start and most of whom had no choice about serving and risking all in it.

"It is now three hours later and I just watched *The Owl and the Pussycat* with Barbara Streisand and George Segal. It was quite funny, even if I was wrapped up in my poncho, as it was raining really hard. After that I went to a floor show, but it was not very good. As usual, the club was filled with pilots. Most of the fliers around here are cavalry troopers. They are directly descended from the old horse soldiers, only now have helicopters as mounts. They wear black Stetsons with crossed sabers on their crowns and are just as boisterous and devil may care as the originals probably were. They fly the gunships and catch a lot of hell and will be the last ones to leave Nam. The bodies we received yesterday were from the 2/17 [2nd Squadron 17th Cavalry Regiment] and those guys were probably at our last show."

I think there was a mutual appreciation among all of the 2/17, 101st Airborne Division, and the 85th Evac staff.

OCT 28. "We've been admitting a lot of patients with just minor stuff lately. We get a lot of a disease called cellulitis. It is a swelling and infection of any kind of skin abrasions and sores. I'm sure it is a result of the moisture and it is very repulsive looking. With the constant rain, we'll be getting a lot of that as well as respiratory infections, not to mention drug abuse and fight injuries—all indirectly related to 100% humidity for so long a time. It's going to be a long winter.

Bill Green got back from the 3rd Field Hospital in Saigon last night. (He had a history of kidney stones, so was sent to Saigon for further tests to determine if his parathyroids were malfunctioning.) He seems to be OK and won't be evaced out, so I'm glad he will be here through our inspections, although I was looking forward to taking his hooch and buying his electric blanket, phone, heater, refrigerator and air conditioner. He gets to go home Dec. 10.

We were all flabbergasted to hear Bill talk about life at the 3rd Field. He said it is a masonry painted building with trimmed lawns and a gymnasium and swimming pool. All offices have carpets and mahogany desks. The admin areas have staff cars (air conditioned) assigned to them (we have an old 2 ½ ton truck and a jeep). The staff wears whites or khakis (we all, including nurses, wear jungle fatigues and boots). Three times a week a chopper takes anyone who wants to go down to Vũng Tàu (Australian in-country rest and recreation site) for water skiing and fishing. Staff can go anywhere in Saigon as long as they wear either khakis or civvies. There are 5 officers clubs—offering nightly entertainment and lobster dinners (we can get ham sandwiches, but no lettuce or tomatoes, and hard-boiled eggs—sometimes).

They have not seen a battle casualty in over 3 months, and their triage area has been converted into a theater. They have elaborate bunkers and massive fence networks (we have some culverts covered with sandbags and four strands of concertina wires). Bill says the worst part of all is their constant complaining about their situation. That is one thing that's sort of peculiar about the 85th. It is just accepted, and you almost never hear complaining about our inconveniences. We just say, "Phu Bai is all right," and that covers it, and everyone knows what you're talking about and shares your sentiments and drops it at that.

What burns me most about this situation over here is the supply system. The people who need things the worst have to fight the hardest to get them, if at all. It took forever to get sandbags to fortify the nurses' area, and we still don't have enough. We hardly have enough vehicles to function, and yet they are congested with cars and jeeps down south. We have 3 Korean War–vintage ambulances out of our fleet of 10 that will run at all, and Bill said they have a whole fleet of shiny new Dodge ambulances in Saigon. We are in the coldest area of Nam in the winter, yet we are allowed one small electric water heater for 35 officers and almost none of us get hot water for showering. Our ER, A&D, and X-Ray areas have been under about an inch of water the last two days because we can't get tar to patch our roofs. There are just too many unscrupulous people and not enough supervision in the supply system. People skim off what they want on the way up until those at the end of the line only get what's left. There are no watches, cameras, tapes, razor blades, refrigerators or recent magazines in Phu Bai, but you can be sure they are available in Long Binh and Saigon.

Forgive my bitching. I feel a little better now. It's a real shame that the Army won't let us switch places halfway through our tours. I've never heard of anyone getting transferred from the 85th—they only get sent to it, apparently. We do have some good and dedicated people here, and the morale is high, and I will be proud to have served with them and at least will be able to say I saw the war. After seeing some of what these grunts up here suffer through, I'd be hesitant to complain if I'd served my tour in Saigon or Long Binh. Bill said the people down there looked at him as though he had just been released from an NVA prison when he told them he was from Phu Bai and that it was only a 10-minute chopper ride from the DMZ."

I remain uncomfortable calling attention to the inequities we experienced at the 85th, especially when compared to those of so many of our combat Soldiers and POWs. However, even after all these years, I would like to ask some of the senior commanders back in Nam how such corruption could have gone unnoticed, unaddressed, uncorrected, and unpunished. What ever happened to "taking care of our troops?" Alas, all those commanders have now passed on, and one more uncomfortable and unanswered question remains on the book of Vietnam. Or perhaps that's just the direction in which all wars eventually evolve.

"We had an unscheduled Filipino floor show tonight. Their equipment and costumes were ragged, but they were great. They played medleys of the Beatles, Beach Boys, the Lettermen, the Temptations, the Platters, Four Seasons, and Jackson Five. As usual, the Cavalry was out in force. They're really something to see. I decided not to drink tonight because I would have to go out in the rain to use the bathroom."

OCT 29. "Thanks so much for the care package I received today. I still don't eat in my room, other than cookies you and Mom send, due to the roaches. I've also been hearing rats in the attic, so I hate to give them any encouragement or temptation.

Our XO spread the word that another typhoon was on the way and had every available person putting sandbags on roofs to keep them from blowing away. I got up on the roof of the registrar's office with one of my PFCs and bagged it this morning. It really tired us out, as the tin roof is steep and the rain just made it more difficult. The bags weigh 25 to 50 lbs. each and we tie from 4 to 6 bags at about 5-foot intervals along a flexible communications wire and then "saddlebag" them over the roof crest. It seems quite effective in keeping the tin from lifting off in the winds. Another typhoon will probably finish this place off, as it's on its last leg anyway. The wards are all surrounded by revetments (hollow walls, 3 ft. wide, filled with dirt) that threaten to collapse, as many are leaning and rotted out now.

I've determined to be in as good shape as you for our R&R and have already just about lost my little (?) roll. But since the gym (hangar) is flooded from Hester, we haven't gotten to play any sports. I haven't minded that too much, though, because I always get hot and sweaty, and then it's the pits to have to get out in the rain to go take a cold shower, and I do mean cold. May I never take hot water and flush toilets for granted again!"

OCT 30. "Today has been the 6th straight day of blowing rain with no letup and the 4th day with no letters. But I did finally get my new camera. I just learned last week that prints are about $4.00 for 12, so I'll probably be having slides made after I learn to use it.

The enclosed article is from *Pacific Stars and Stripes*, an armed forces newspaper that caters to U.S. forces in the Pacific theater. It is daily, so we can stay a little current about what is going on in the world. The dustoff crew in the article flies out of here about every third week. There are usually four crews of four that spend a week at a time up here. They are based at Red Beach in Da Nang, though. The Lt. Livingston in the article is a friend of mine, an MSC (there seems to be a fair number of MSC officers flying dustoffs). He is very quiet and has a serious demeanor. We've talked some about the U. of Wyoming since I applied for graduate school there."

OCT 31. "The only interesting admit we had today was a 7-year-old VN boy who had been hit by a jeep. He had a broken leg and fractured pelvis as well as some really severe lacerations on both legs. Once again, his dad brought him here because he knew the Americans would provide the best care. They know to go to the MPs with trouble because they always come straight to us, even though they know Vietnamese are supposed to go to Hue. The doctor told me he was glad they came here, though, because he doesn't get to do much pediatrics but had experience with this kind of injuries, so the kid would be much better off here. Even though we hurt a lot of these people, we sure help a lot more. A new high school is being built just up the road from here with donations of equipment, time, and money from GIs here in Phu Bai."

Dear Janie

The 'Dustoff' Men
Fly In, Fly Out... It's a Race With Death

By HOLGER JENSEN

RED BEACH, Vietnam (AP) — An ammunition boat blows up on a GI's head at a dirty little fire base called Rawhide. Twenty miles away four young men, dragged from sleep by a whistle blast, steer their helicopter through rain squalls. It is after midnight, a lonely time to fly.

Running lights are doused as the chopper "approaches Rawhide. "Nighthawk" gunships are arriving. Rawhide gunners are alerted to the presence of the "friendly" helicopter and the danger of collision is very real. But red lights make a target for Viet Cong sharpshooters in the surrounding hills.

The aircraft drops blindly into an inky void and someone mutters on the intercom: "Christ, it's dark."

Suddenly light flickers thinly on the ridgetop below. Rawhide has switched on truck headlights to show the chopper the pad, and the chopper homes in. Before the skids touch earth, stretcher bearers are running forward.

The patient is given first aid as the helicopter claws skyward again. Fifteen minutes later he is at the 95th Evacuation Hospital in Da Nang and the aerial ambulancemen of Dustoff 608 are homeward bound to Red Beach.

They will never know the patient's name nor if they saved his life. But they will go to sleep satisfied, mission accomplished.

What the U.S. Army calls "Dustoff" is one of the most awesome developments of modern warfare. Medical evacuation by helicopter assures hospital care for every soldier

bumped into two men who appeared to be Viet Cong.

"I've got plenty of time, I'm still young," he says. "When I didn't shoot me," he says. "I like to think they showed compassion. Just as I would have. I've never fired a gun at anyone in Vietnam. I'm not here to hurt anyone. I consider myself a conscientious objector in a different part of the war."

Dustoff doesn't approve of Lopez's involvement, but Americans, he calls himself a Universalist, refers to the Viet Cong as "individuals," rather than United States "had a job to do here but the time to go home was two years ago." Meeks concedes the war "hasn't been fought right, but those demonstrators burn me up. Will Twice Lopez has risked his life by jumping off his helicopter in enemy terrain to search for wounded GIs. One time he wears an American flag on his flying suit and declares: "We've done the right thing

and we're getting out the right way."

As the war abates, the men of Dustoff 608 find themselves picking up fewer combat casualties and more victims of accidents, illness and drug overdoses. In one 36-hour period they evacuated the injured GI from Rawhide, another GI suffering burns, and five Vietnamese, two soldiers with suspected typhoid, a civilian injured in a traffic accident, a soldier with suspected meningitis and a woman with chest pains.

"I can remember when one chopper averaged six to eight wounded a day," said Meeks. "Now it's more like 12 a week, sometimes less when there aren't any operations going on. Most of our combat casualties are caused by booby traps now—they're the worst kind."

The 236th Medical Detachment, based at Red Beach, 109 miles north of Da Nang, has seven helicopters serving three critical northern provinces. Last January the unit carried 913 patients, in September 383. But air crews spend more flying time covering greater distances, and thus take more risks, than the closest thing to a milk run is a blood run —ferrying blood where it is needed, fast.

So far this year, eight Medicopters flying out of Red Beach have suffered damage from ground fire or mines that detonated under their skids.

"You're damn right we're proud," said Livingston. "We consider ourselves special because we fly missions others don't fly."

in Vietnam within 3 minutes of sickness or injury.

But there is never a shortage of volunteers to fly the unarmed birds with the red crosses.

Men who fly this lifeline see the worst side of the war—the wounded, the fever-ridden, the maimed and the dead, they take risks that become magnified as the war winds down.

Lt. Scott Livingston, 24, of Cody, Wyo., is the aircraft commander of Dustoff 608. Eleven months and 600 combat hours over Vietnam have inured him to the horrors of war, but he still gets "the greatest feeling in the world" when a wounded patient gives him a smile or a thumbs-up sign.

A sociology graduate of the University of Wyoming, Livingston was last shot at last month at Pleiku. He only has a month left in Vietnam and he worries every time he flies. But he goes on flying because "you know someone down there needs help."

Al, 29, pilot WO Walter Meeks, of Danville, Va., is the oldest crewman. He entered the Army as a 17-year-old high school dropout and spent one term in Vietnam before taking infantry training. He is married with two children.

"I know what it's like fighting on the ground," he says. "When some of my people got hit and a Dustoff came in, I'd get tears in my eyes. I was so thankful I wanted to be one of them. I wanted to arouse that emotion in others."

Crew Chief Willert Wills, Kilgore, Tex., is only 21 but he feels he has grown up in Vietnam. Wills enlisted in the Army straight out of high school, extended three times to remain in the war zone, has been shot up three times in flight, and shot down once. Recently he signed

Medic Anthony Lopez, 27, Dallas, Tex., entered the Army with an anthropology degree from Southern Methodist University. He calls himself a pacifist, refers to his participation in a clear conscience.

Pacific Stars & Stripes 7
Friday, Oct. 29, 1971

126

November 1971

NOV 1. "I learned today that Sgt. McLemore (my NCO) will probably be all right, so I won't lose him after all. Bill Green decided today to go ahead and turn registrar over to me, and he will merely advise me until he leaves in December. Captain Burt Wilde comes up in two weeks and will apparently take over my job as Asst. Registrar and A&D Officer. Can you believe I'll have a captain working under me (even if he does know more)?

As for your questions, we have no ARVN troops on the compound. They do have a base camp and basic training reservation just down the highway. They fire off machine guns and firecrackers every now and then which makes us jump until we determine its them. We do have a lot of Vietnamese civilians working for us as KPs, hooch maids, interpreters, etc. Occasionally, we have an ARVN crew member on our dustoffs to act as interpreter since we pick up almost all the ARVN casualties. The dustoff that crashed last month had all U.S. crew members."

NOV 2. "P.S. I almost forgot to brag on Shannon. Sounds like her learning is almost out of control. We must have an extremely sharp kid, huh?"

NOV 4. "We did well on our inspection, although there were a few discrepancies with our records. Therefore, today I spent most of my time reviewing the clinical records of GIs who had died at the 85th last year. Actually, it was surprising how few had died here, although several expired after being evaced to other hospitals. It's amazing how much the body can endure and still live and then again how little it takes to kill sometimes. We lost a 22-year-old yesterday to a ruptured vessel in the base of his brain. His death certificate was typed up several hours before his death, it was such a certainty. He died within 24 hours of the rupture. Yet, I came across the record today of a kid who had lost the entire lower half of his pelvis, one arm, and an eye, and yet lived for five days and was alert and talking for a while."

I also remember an ARVN that was brought to us to help him die peacefully. His entire lower body, including his pelvis, was blown away. I don't recall how long he lingered, but it was an unforgettable sight—seeing his lower abdomen packed with gauze. He was very young. A sight I shall never forget.

NOV 5. "Early this morning we received the body of an E-5 with 4 gunshot wounds. He had apparently been fooling around and thrown a smoke grenade under the hooch of an E-6. He came out immediately with an M16 and shot him dead in his tracks. I don't blame him if the guy wasn't a friend. Everyone is so jumpy with all the drug freaks and neurotics over here; the guy was asking for trouble in the worst way. A few times, guys passing my hooch have thrown rocks or cans at it, probably assuming no one was inside, but it makes me jump about 3 feet high. I guess everyone is a little trigger happy in a war zone.

This afternoon a lieutenant was brought in (patients on dustoffs are typically laying on canvas stretchers called litters and are transferred to gurneys on the landing pad and wheeled into the ER) with the crew chief giving him closed heart massage. The ER crew took over and brought him back, but he almost surely suffered brain damage. He had touched a 220-volt wire with his elbow and went into cardiac arrest. He was burned in several places, but they didn't look like burns from a flame look.

I was amazed they got him going again, as he had that pale greenish color and his eyes were already rolled back in a blank stare. But they suctioned the gunk from his lungs, hooked him up to oxygen, and shocked him and he cranked back up. He was placed in ICU and was still unconscious when I left."

NOV 6. "We've stopped getting so many patients and hopefully our census will go back down. We have 74 as of yesterday, with only one battle casualty left. It's been over a week since we've gotten any and it seems sort of strange that things are so quiet, especially with 7 straight days of sunshine. The only thing that remains constant is the number of drug addicts we keep admitting.

Last Wednesday everyone assigned to the hospital had to take a urine test—actually, I think everyone in Phu Bai had to take one. I suppose the purpose is to pinpoint the users and pushers and to discourage others. Yesterday, a sergeant and I searched a couple of wards, since a vial of heroin had been found. We didn't find any more, but we did discover a patient who had not turned in all his money when admitted. We take almost all their money so they won't have it get stolen or be able to buy drugs once admitted.

I went over to Bill Green's hooch tonight, drank a couple of beers and listened to about half of the *Jesus Christ Superstar* soundtrack. It was very interesting and seems to be becoming a sensation over here."

NOV 7. "I cringe with the thought of searching for a job and a place to live and moving again when this is all over. I try not to dwell on it and know there is nothing I can do about it now, but still those things are always in the back of my mind.

The war seems to have started again, as we got in several casualties. I didn't work today, so don't know the stories behind them or how bad the injuries were. I do know two choppers went down and we treated the crew of one of them for minor wounds, but I don't think we've heard from the other crew. This evening a Huey came in with 2 men clinging to a cable about 100 ft below it. I'll bet there is an interesting story behind that little incident. Almost all these crew members have harrowing tales if they have been here any length of time at all.

As for my telling you things that go on over here, none of it is classified to my knowledge. About the only classified stuff the registrar gets involved with are lists of important people who must be reported if hospitalized. These include relatives of government officials, generals, Medal of Honor recipients, etc. Also, casualties often come in with secret papers that we take charge of until someone from their unit can come and sign for them. These usually involve codes, maps and plans, lists of strengths and equipment, etc."

NOV 8. "I am AOD tonight and it just stopped raining, so hoping it stays stopped. We are having another floor show tonight. We treated a Korean band member for appendicitis and are accepting the show as payment. That is another of my new duties—accounting and charging of civilian payments. There are a lot of U.S. firms over here, and we treat them just as though we were a commercial hospital. They are billed $61/day for hospitalization and $13/visit on an outpatient basis."

NOV 10. "We had two deaths last night, which kept us pretty busy today. One of them was the Lt. that got shocked by the hot wire. The other was a 'skag freak' (heroin addict) that developed septicemia (a type of blood poisoning) from unsterile needles. He came in yesterday evening and was dead within 3 hours. Deaths generate a lot of work for us, as we must notify USARV Casualty in Long Binh (Saigon) for further notification of kin, notify the Chaplain, call Graves Registration to pick up the body, prepare autopsy requests (when required) and have them signed by the CO, be sure all death certificates and other reports are properly prepared, plus a few other minor details.

Yesterday a doctor asked me to go out to the dead shed and help him complete a death certificate on a GI. He was very stiff and had been shot through the right cheek with an M16. I had to put my arms under his back and neck and lift so the doctor could look for other wounds. The bullet had blown out the back of his skull and I got brains and blood all over my arms. Turns out he was returning to his perimeter after relieving himself. It was right at dark and a Puerto Rican kid had just assumed his sentry position and gave the challenge password when he saw him approaching from the brush. Apparently, the accent was heavy enough that the deceased didn't understand and kept coming, so he got shot. At least that was the story we got from the dustoff that brought him in. Typical of war!

Also, last night, we received a Capt. and a First Sgt. who had been shot by one of the men in their company, so the CID (criminal investigation division) was in and out getting statements and copies of records, etc. all day. Yesterday the MPs brought in a lineup for a warrant officer to pick out the addict who stabbed him in the heart. He is being medivaced tomorrow. Seems like we're doing ourselves more harm than the enemy, since we've only received one battle casualty in 10 days now.

Since there has been so little action lately, things have been getting more and more irritating. We've been getting a lot of static about reports, who we can air evac, haircuts, uniforms, etc. I don't think we can get out of this environment soon enough. The more these guys are harassed and the less they have to do, the more they drink and shoot up heroin and the more trouble they get in.

Bill Green just told me that the hospital XO had finally decided that I was to be the new registrar. There had been some question about it since Burt was more experienced and Regular Army (He is a career officer. I'm a reserve officer), although I am more senior in grade. This will be a lot of responsibility but should be good experience for me."

NOV 11. "I love our little Shannon so much, and yet I already wonder how she will turn out and how good we as parents will rate in the long run.

We got no BCs, murders, fraggings, suicides, or drug overdoses today, so I stayed busy reading regulations and trying to learn all I can before Bill leaves."

NOV 12. "Still no word on the 101st standing down. You may read about this hospital closing before we know it ourselves, at this rate. I do know that the 91st closed at the same time the Americal Division pulled out, and quite possibly we will do the same—but if we are going to do that, we should have heard by now. Possibly we will be cut in size and left as a sort of dispensary, in which case I may or may not get stuck here until the bitter end. Nobody who knows says, and the ones who don't know speculate and start rumors.

Still no BCs, even though the weather is holding pretty well. We did have to send our dustoff out four times last night to pick up 15 ARVN litter patients and take them to the Hue hospital. They must have gotten into some bad stuff somewhere."

NOV 13. "I've been playing some basketball and touch football with mostly enlisted guys. It's really nice not to be under the pressure of command and to be able to relax and get along with the EM. I'm sure most of our black soldiers have very little use for officers and NCOs, but they accept us that play ball with them. It's fun to watch them when they really let it all hang out in the gym and forget about race and officers and the Army. When I've played football with the EM a few times, they've told me I still get around pretty good for a fellow getting along in years. That's kinda hard to take from 19 and 20 year-olds.

There was always palpable racial tension on our grounds, and probably everywhere else, especially as the war was winding down. The Black Soldiers did a thing called "dapping" that I never understood and found a little annoying at the time. It seemed to be some kind of secret hand jive and was exchanged almost like a religious ritual whenever two or more Black Soldiers were walking past each other. I googled it recently and it makes more sense now with the war in the retrospective rearview mirror:

According to *Folklife* magazine on community, social justice dated September 22, 2014, "Dap is an acronym for 'dignity and pride' whose movements translate to 'I'm not above you; you're not above me; we're side by side; we're together.' Dap was a symbol of solidarity and served as a substitute for the Black Power salute prohibited by the military."

These days, I readily will walk up to a Black man wearing a Vietnam veteran cap. I tell him, "Welcome home, brother!" I've never not had my salutation returned. We all bled the same color. For years I was reticent to wear a VN veteran cap, not wanting to call attention to myself. In time, I have learned that vets will readily talk to other veterans who initiate a conversation. Having the common ground of a war experience makes it easier to talk to a stranger. We know the questions to ask.

NOV 14. "I got letters today from Uncle Lickey, Aunt Janice, David, and Phil Smith, along with a *Daily Texan*. I also got my acceptance notice from SFASU. I thought I had things all clear in my mind, but I've laid on my bunk for 4 hours hashing it out. I've about decided to go ahead and apply for the early out, although the thought of exams and money pressures make me cringe, but yet I can't see passing up the chance to get back to you. If we're not planning to stay in the Army, I feel like I'm just spinning my wheels over here."

NOV 15. "I will put in my request for early out tomorrow and get Burt to carry it to Da Nang for me as he is going that way to Long Binh for a conference. The XO said he would recommend approval and then remarked, "You can see how much we think of you, can't you?" and chuckled a little. Actually, I guess if we thought much of each other, he wouldn't have approved it. We were both thinking "good riddance," probably."

NOV 17. "I didn't write last night and instead wrote a long letter to David. Sometimes I'm afraid of what he might do. The stress of his situation, what with the squabbling, the debts, and the school, must be unimaginable, and I bragged on the way he is standing up to it and meant every word of it.

Today I was told that there are no provisions for MSCs to get more than a 90 day drop for school and that I might as well forget it! Our personnel officer spent the entire morning working on it and finally called our next higher HQ, and they couldn't find any authorization either. I called the 67th Medical Group (our command group) last week and was told to go ahead and put in my request, that I would be the first one to try, and it might get approved since troop strength was being cut.

We had a slight racial incident last night. It was all over a Vietnamese prostitute that had been snuck into the compound. It resulted in a white pulling an M16 on several blacks. My hooch mate, Capt. Bodie got it all settled. Then today, the main black involved walked up and smashed the white and pounded him severely. As it stands now, the white won't press charges, as he is a short-timer. Hopefully, this will all go away. I just hope this is not a sign of more trouble ahead.

Also today, a chopper came in with a man dangling 100 ft below on a cable. It turned out he was a CCN (Command & Control North. Vietnamese involved in highly classified Special Operations). He was possibly a North Vietnamese, because he looked Korean, he was so different from the South Vietnamese. He was much larger and had a wider face. He spoke good English, though. He had been shot, but his radio deflected the bullet and it barely nipped his leg. An American adviser followed him in and wouldn't tell me where it happened but did say he had ridden like that for about 25 miles (probably Laos or DMZ area). The weather is cool and clear today, and the guy was almost frozen. We bundled him up, and he shivered for 20 minutes before he could stop, and his color changed from purple back to normal. Don't see many cold weather victims here."

NOV 18. "I've worked from 9:00 until 4:30 today and finally found the obscure directive that explains the policy that seems to imply that I am eligible for an early drop. Now it's a matter of whether the application must go through Dept of Army in D.C., or can be processed in Nam, and if so whether the information can be sent and received from Long Binh (USARV HQ) in time. Please send the transcripts back to me, as I plan to apply to vet school from here.

I thought you might get a kick out of the article that was in the *Stars and Stripes* today. It explains pretty well the saying "Phu Bai is all right," which is generally synonymous with "Phu Bai sucks," which is also heard frequently. It is known and used all over the northern section of VN. After the typhoon, our XO sent a telegram to the 67th Medical Group that said only "Phu Bai is all right." We all thought it was hilarious. I have ordered matching sweatshirts for us with the slogan on back and 85th Evac Hosp on the front. [We still have those sweatshirts, yet they are a bit snug!]

A "slick" bringing in 3 CCNs, all with bullet wounds.

Letters Home from 85th Evacuation Hospital Vietnam, 1971

A Half-Inch From the DMZ

Phu Bai, They Say, Is All Right... Mostly

By SPEC. 5 RAY CHESNUT

Waiting on the hard stand at Cam Ranh Bay, the "newbee" is apprehensive. "When I call out your name," the loudspeaker blares, "answer up loud and clear and fall out to the right of this building."

He yawns as the voice calls off name after name. "Not another night in this place," he thinks.

Then it happens: his name is called. "Here!" he screams. "Ohmagosh, wonder where I'm going. It can't be Pleiku, they already called that."

"The group whose names I've just called," the speaker says, "are going to Phu Bai. That's Fooooo Bye. Fall out and get your gear. Be ready for a zero-three-hundred flight."

Rushing out the gate, he stops in front a large map. "Phu Bai, Phu Bai, does that start with an F? Let's see... Oh no, it's only a half-an-inch from the DMZ — I'd better go have a beer."

At the club after two or three beers, he gathers his courage. At the end of the bar stands a short-timer with faded fatigues, red boots and knowledge oozing from every pore.

"Excuse me," the green one says, "I just got my assignment and I wonder if you could tell me something about it?"

"Sure, kid. Hey baby-san! Bring me two beers! Now then, where ya going?"

"Phu Bai."

"Phu Bai? I just came from there. Listen, kid, you're lucky—Phu Bai is all right! Two more beers! Let me tell you about Phu Bai.

"Nobody knows how it got started, but it's there. Ask anyone about the place and they'll tell you. When you get off the plane up there, there's a big sign that says "Welcome to Phu Bai, home of the 26th General Support Group and the 101st Airborne Division (Airmobile) — Phu Bai is all right!

"Legend has it that Hanoi Hanna started the whole thing when she used to say something like this at the close of her show: 'Tonight, Dong Ha, Quang Tri, and Camp Eagle will take rockets, but Phu Bai is all right — for now.'

"For the grunts in the field it is almost Stateside, and for those who live there it is better than the bush. I guess it's far enough north that they don't care more about the job you do than how you look. But, no matter how you look at it, Phu Bai is all right.

"But, I got to warn you, kid. The war is winding down and they are starting to crack down on the Stateside regs. It's getting so a lot of us old-timers think Phu Bai is all right, but not as all right as it used to be."

"Well, thanks a lot, fella," the newfer says. "You've taken a nell of a load off my mind."

When he gets back to the group he tells everyone. "Hey, wow, fellas, we're going to Phu Bai! Ya wanna hear about Phu Bai?"

Same 3 CCNs being unloaded onto gurneys to be rolled into the ER for treatment of hypothermia and gunshot wounds.

This afternoon, a slick brought in 3 more CCNs hanging onto a rope ladder. Another slick came in a few minutes later with one hanging from a cable. All were about frozen and all had been shot—not the usual fragmentation wounds we are used to, so they were undoubtedly in some close combat. It sure makes me wonder what's happening out there that is so intense the choppers can't land long enough to drag the injured onboard. Only one of them had been seriously injured of the four. I marvel when I see men like these, that lead lives consisting of such extreme danger day after day. I'll bet not one in twenty lives to see old age all in one piece. They go until they are either killed or lose arms and/or legs and can't go anymore."

NOV 19. "Your description of Shannon going to the cupboard and asking "pees" [please] and "muk" [milk] really got to me.

I learned today that my drop request would have to be approved in the Surgeon General's Office in Washington. That would take at least 3–4 months. I guess that's a disadvantage of being an MSC, because combat officers get their approvals in Nam. Also, one of our doctors told me that our CO had been drinking heavily last night and had confided to him that the hospital was now scheduled to close April 15. My chances of getting out early are down to + or – none."

NOV 20. "Occasionally I even wonder if getting out is still the right thing to do with so few jobs available, and now that captain pay is going up to $14,000 per year.

We had some more weird accident victims today. In one case, 2 GIs were testing the armament system on the rocket launcher of a Cobra gunship just across the runway from us. A rocket fired somehow and went sideways through one and then through the chest of the other. Both were killed instantly. The rocket glanced off a revetment and apparently never exploded—just disappeared. Both GIs had clean holes through them about the size of a fist.

This afternoon a guy was brought in who was disassembling the fuse of an artillery round when it exploded. He was extremely lucky, as it did no permanent damage to his eyes or face other than a few cuts. It split several fingers, but he won't lose any.

This morning (2:00 a.m.) a soldier came in who had been hit in the head with a machete, but it didn't hurt him very badly. So it goes, on and on."

NOV 22. "The Vietnamese civilians are getting pretty worried about their jobs with us pulling out. I heard there was a demonstration in Chu Lai last night because there are no jobs now with the Americal Division and the 91st leaving.

Headquarters, ARVN Hospital in Hue

ARVN patients at the Hue hospital. Open air rooms and poor sanitation.

We told the provincial hospital in Hue today that we would no longer see any VN patients unless it was a life-saving emergency. Their attitude toward sick or injured really amazes me. Yesterday, a missionary came to ask if we would look at an old man who was comatose after his motorbike flipped. He was taken to the hospital in Hue and laid there for over 12 hours without a single doctor stopping to look at him. Seems like that hospital is just a place to go to either die or get better, with little help in either direction. The old man seems to be getting better now."

NOV 23. "FYI, for peace of mind in knowing I had done all possible to get the drop, I sent my request on through channels even though I've been told there is no way. Also, I sent a personal registered letter with copies of my request and SFA acceptance to the head man in charge of MSC drops in Washington and asked him to expedite matters if he could and would."

Looking back now, I wonder how I even got his name and address.

"Your mother's letter was greatly appreciated and she said some very sweet things that meant a lot to me. I feel very fortunate to have your parents as in-laws.

Today has been somewhat out of the ordinary. To begin with, I had to relieve one of my radio operators from duty. He reported for his shift drunk last night. I had been thinking of taking him off for some time as he had been getting little sleep and seemed increasingly excitable on the radio. I've also been concerned about the lack of sleep another of our operators has been getting. The responsibility seems to weigh quite heavily on them and worries them subconsciously, as well it might. An incident occurred last year in which the radio operator got flustered and took down the wrong map coordinates on a dustoff request. He sent the ship to a hostile fire zone instead and it got shot down.

DEPARTMENT OF THE ARMY
85TH EVACUATION HOSPITAL (SMBL)
APO SAN FRANCISCO 96308

AVBJ-GC-EC-R   22 NOV 71

COL. E.R. MCCANDLESS
CHIEF, PERSONNEL & TRAINING DIVISION
OFFICE OF THE SURGEON GENERAL
DEPARTMENT OF THE ARMY
WASHINGTON, D.C. 20315

Dear Col. McCandless;

I am inclosing a copy of my request for early release from active duty in order to attend school.

The original copy of the request is presently being forwarded through channels.

Due to slow dissemination of information in Vietnam as well as the recency of the authorizing directives, I have only lately become aware of the early release program as it applies in my case. For this reason my request is being sent in at this late date.

Any assistance you might lend in the expeditious processing of my application would be greatly appreciated.

                                                    Sincerely Yours,

                                                    JAMES G. SLACK
2 Incl   CPT   MSC
1. Ltr of acceptance
2. Request for early out

This afternoon one of our two hospital dustoff choppers was destroyed. It was on a mission to pick up 11 ARVNs who had been shot about 1-1/2 miles south of the DMZ. It had landed on the pad at Fire Base Fuller and was about to load patients when a mortar hit beneath its tail boom. It began to shudder and buck uncontrollably and finally lifted and smashed its nose into the pad. The pilot said as it was bucking, an ARVN LTC failed to get out of the way, and the rotor blade hit him. He said the guy seemed to explode and he remembered seeing his head fly off. Our crew of four all jumped out just before the Huey exploded and burned. I wish I had had a recorder with me as I listened to the whole story unfold on the radio. Another dustoff was sent in but not permitted to land until Cobras had been called in to work the area over. There were several of us huddled around the radio just as though we were listening to a ball game.

It is really dream-like and hard to realize the things that can happen. I had been playing volleyball every day with the crew of that chopper and it seems so strange that those friends could so easily be killed in their everyday job."

To this day I still remember how wired our pilots were when they arrived back at the 85th. They couldn't sit still, and their eyes were like BBs. I doubt they got much sleep that night. They had lots of adrenaline pumping for a while.

"We had originally tried to get the ARVNs at Hue to fly up there since they were closer and these were their soldiers, but they couldn't locate their pilots. That gives some idea of the incompetency we face in many areas of Vietnamization. Our crews will be airborne within 5–7 minutes at any time, day or night."

NOV 24. "Bad weather (blowing, chilling, constant rain) today is sort of bittersweet for us, for it means we will have trouble sending out patients who need to go, and yet it also means the crews won't be flying. Three or four of our nurses who are married to pilots rejoice every time the weather gets bad, even though we are all miserable.

A mouse just ran across my floor! The roaches seem to be on the increase, but that's the first mammal I've actually seen in here. My EM have been telling me about waking up to rats running across their chests. It's hilarious to hear them tell their well-embellished stories.

I'm not quite sure what to tell your mom about quoting me to a congressman. I don't know what she wants to say and tell them that they don't already know or what they would or could do with the information.

There is no artillery firing tonight. This is the first night I can remember that I haven't heard a few rounds at least. The night before last I was awakened by bombing over in the A Shau Valley. That was a first. From all I've read and heard, we are now trying to blast the supply routes coming down along the Laos/VN border. A 101st pilot told me tonight that no more patrols should be going out after next week. Here's hoping."

Medevac Copter Downed After DMZ Battle; 1 Dead

S&S Vietnam Bureau

SAIGON — A unit from the 1st ARVN Inf. Div. tangled with Communists Tuesday near the Demilitarized Zone, and a U.S. Army UH1 medevac helicopter was shot down in the same area, allied spokesmen said Wednesday.

The 1st ARVN Div. infantrymen killed seven Reds but lost two men killed and 11 wounded in the clash 22 miles west-northwest of Quang Tri, the South Vietnamese command said.

The fight broke out Tuesday morning near Dong Ha Mountain, five miles from the DMZ, and the medevac chopper was shot down in the same area Tuesday afternoon.

The U.S. command said the green medevac copter was hit as it hovered over a wounded ARVN soldier. The South Vietnamese soldier was killed when the helicopter crashed on top of him. There were no U.S. casualties.

U.S. Air Force B52 bombers flew two missions in Quang Tri Province, and U.S. Navy gunners fired at targets in the DMZ, according to spokesmen.

One flight of B52s hit bunkers and antiaircraft positions 28 miles southwest of Quang Tri, and another formation of the eight-engine bombers struck antiaircraft sites and storage depots 12 miles southeast of Khe Sanh.

The command also said it would support the South Vietnamese thrust against Communist sanctuaries in Cambodia with planes and helicopters.

At least two divisions of South Vietnamese airborne, Ranger, infantry and armored cavalry elements are now involved in the Cambodia operation, which began Monday.

Fighting was sporadic elsewhere in Vietnam, and 7th AF fighter-bombers flew only four tactical air strikes in the country, spokesmen said. Elements from the 7th ARVN Inf. Div. killed 16 Communists and captured one in scattered skirmishes in the Delta's Dinh Tuong, Kien Hoa and Vinh Binh provinces, according to spokesmen. Two ARVN soldiers were wounded.

South Vietnamese Rangers killed 11 Reds and captured one 20 miles southwest of Da Nang, and a Regional Forces company killed nine Communists in the central highlands seven miles northeast of Kontum, spokesmen said. There were no South Vietnamese casualties in either clash.

Pacific Stars & Stripes, Friday, Nov. 26, 1971

NOV 25. "Today is Thanksgiving, and fortunately I got two letters from you, 18th and 19th. Today has been about like any other, only with a tremendous turkey dinner—for which the officers had to pay $1.00 instead of the usual $0.55. EM don't pay for meals. [Officers in a combat theater received a subsistence allowance of $47.88 per month in 1971, and EM did not.]

I'm glad I worked today to keep me occupied. I kept thinking of last Thanksgiving. Remember how I missed the big buck and got my thumb slammed in the action of my shotgun? It was clear and frosty that morning. Then we took our little 4 mo. old baby in her cradle seat and went out to the Fenesy's parents' farm in South Carolina for lunch. That day was probably one of the best we had in Georgia."

The Fenesy's parents had a tradition of inviting a family that was away from home to share Thanksgiving with them each year. It meant so much to us!

"As for some of your questions, the baby boy was sent to the 95th [This referred to a five-day old premature baby boy who wouldn't eat, and had difficulty breathing. I had previously written to Janie about him.] I don't know what happened there.

There are many U.S. contractor firms over here who handle the engineering type work—electrical systems, power, plumbing, building, etc. Their workers sign contracts for 6 mo.–1 year, I think, and come over to work. They make fabulous money and get officers' club and PX privileges. We usually have one or two in the hospital at any one time.

There are also a lot of Korean civilians here, too, as well as soldiers. They are famous for their toughness and merciless attitude towards communists, but yet unpopular among GIs for their practice of buying out our PXs and then shipping the stuff home for resale. I read a quote from a U.S. officer in which he said, "If we really wanted to win this war, we would put all Koreans down in the Delta and a fully stocked PX up in Phu Bai and tell them to go get it."

NOV 27. "Sorry I didn't write last night. We had our final basketball game and a long movie (*Krakatoa, East of Java*), so I decided to let one night pass. We played the only unbeaten team left and lost 91–68, which wasn't as bad as expected. I scored 10 points.

Burt will work out fine. He seems to be a "go-getter" and knows his stuff.

I've been very busy in the Registrar Office learning as much as I can from Bill before he leaves next week. Burt spends most of his time in A&D, since he has taken over my job, except as communications officer, which I remained.

Yesterday a Mohawk OV-1, which is an electronic surveillance/reconnaissance plane, crashed shortly after takeoff here. Both crew members were killed. The pilot had a twin brother who is in the same company and flies the same type plane. I don't know why it crashed, but it occurred just at dawn and it was drizzling and overcast.

I threw in the clippings because they are vaguely related to what we do. Camp Campbell, along with Camp Hochmuth, make up the Phu Bai Combat Base. Many of us at the hospital gave money towards the high school. We also gave some materials for it. We give a lot of our outdated drugs to the Hue hospital, also.

The other clipping concerns our chopper that crashed, although the story in print is different from the one I got from the crew. I know all the pilots dread flying missions up near the DMZ.

Since the U.S. is pulling out, we got orders not to accept any more VN civilian patients unless it is to save life, limb, or sight, or unless they were injured by U.S. troops. That has basically always been the policy, but we always stretched it. Today an 18-year-old was brought in by a missionary. One of our doctors, Cpt. Mike Miller, diagnosed him with leukemia. Mike got our CO's permission to admit him, and Mike will then pay his way down to Saigon to a better equipped VN hospital since the kid's family has no money and the hospital up here could do little for him. As it turned out, Mike's wife of three years died of leukemia two years ago. He felt this kid might have a chance if he got the right treatment. I hadn't known that of Mike, but had always thought of him as being rather subdued and extremely serious about his medicine.

I'm so glad I have a loving wife to come back to. I wonder how many of these men have the kind of love waiting for them that I have. I feel very fortunate to have you and your love for me. May I always be deserving of you, Dearest."

Dear Janie

Chaplain plans new high school

CAMP CAMPBELL, — A formal education is an important asset in today's modern world and it is something many people are denied simply because the money, teachers and the facilities are lacking. Within the Republic of Vietnam there are many fine schools, but even here the need for an education far exceeds the available facilities.

Chaplain (CPT.) Marvin McRoberts, 101st Administrative Co. 101st Airborne Division (Airmobile), plans to fill some of the need around Phu Bai Combat Base with a fund raising drive for a high school in the area.

The site of the proposed facility is at the Nan Duc School in Phu Loung village, eight miles southeast of Hue. The head of the school, Pastor Nguyen Van Na, or Pastor Jonah as he is known by many, is the impetus and originator of the plan to build the high school.

Pastor Jonah left an associate pastorate position in Hue to come to Phu Loung in 1967, to develop a badly-needed church and school in the area.

The first construction consisted of three elementary school rooms completed in 1967 by the 159th Avn. Gp. The church was completed in 1968 with missionary funds and the elementary school was completed in 1969 with aid from the 101ist's 2nd Bde.

The seven room school accommodates 500 children daily, but upon graduation from the sixth grade these children are stymied with no place to go for additional schooling. McRoberts hopes to alleviate this problem by raising enough funds so that Pastor Jonah can complete this school.

"We first became involved in this project this past summer," said McRoberts. "I felt the troops in the company needed an outlet to get them off base and meet some people, and at the same time be of some help to the people other than in their military capacity."

"With the aid of Maj. John Wolfe, commanding officer of the 101st Administrative Company, who provided transportation and other assistance, we started weekly work parties to Phu Loung School," continued the chaplain. "We built swings, teeter-totters, black boards, raised a flagpole and repaired many of the buildings that had been damaged by typhoon and monsoon weather."

The school itself is completely indigeneous and self supporting but because many of the children are war orphans and pay no tuition, very little money can be saved for Pastor Jonah's project.

"We hope to set up booths this coming pay day and rely on the generosity of the soldiers to help us through," said McRoberts.

Pastor Jonah, who has been the target of several communist assassination plots over the years, best expressed the spirit behind the project at the flag raising that was held recently. A mixed group of Vietnamese, Montagnards and South Vietnamese flag was run up the pole and fluttered proudly in the breeze.

"The three stripes of the flag represent the north, south and the middle of our country", said Pastor Jonah. "The color yellow is for our flesh and the red color for our blood. We must bleed everyday for peace."

152

NOV 28. "One of the guys in my office got a real live spruce tree in the mail, so we are having a decorating party tonight. It may not get to be the drunken fest we wanted, though, as this afternoon contact was lost with a Chinook (CH-47) from across the runway. It had 30 GIs on board, and all available choppers including our two went out to search for it, but the weather was so bad all were called back.

We geared up for a mass casualty ("mass cal") situation and are all on standby in the event it is found. We have a big pile of emergency medical supplies on a litter in the ER. A doctor and several medics are on alert to be flown to the crash site if it is found. The Chinook was headed toward Da Nang through the Hai Van pass. It is almost always clouded over this time of year and often our birds are turned back there due to the lack of visibility."

We did not typically receive casualties from air crashes, since they were invariably DOA and were delivered straight to Graves Registration upon recovery. I can only remember receiving a couple of crash victims. They had not been found for a few days and were brought in in pieces zipped up in body bags along with lots of maggots. All we got of one was his hand and wrist. He was identifiable because his watch was still strapped on. A very unpleasant and sad sight.

NOV 29. "I got the portraits of Shannon today. I felt a physical pain when I looked at them for the first time. I think they are really terrific and yet a little sad in that they so clearly show that the baby I left is now a little girl. But what a doll she is!

That Chinook still hasn't been found and we are still on alert. The weather was bad all day, so the search was limited.

I went to the EM club with Bill Green tonight because they were having an Australian floor show, but an NCO asked us to leave since enlisted aren't allowed in our officers' club. I went back later and watched it from a window. That's only the second show I've seen with performers that spoke intelligible English and they were pretty good.

You asked what a CCN &/or mercenary was. Very little is said about them, but I think they are usually VN who work directly under U.S. control. They are trained and paid by us, and they do extremely dangerous work—often behind or among the NVA, and maybe even in North Vietnam.

We learned in a briefing today that Migs (enemy jets) have been flying over us quite frequently lately. I thought I should tell you before you heard it on the news, if it even is released to the news. I don't know what they're doing, probably reconnaissance, but it's a cinch they don't dare fire on us since our air power is so superior.

The cassette tapes I stocked up on at the PX all seem to be defective. They probably knew that when they shipped them up here to us."

NOV 30. "We were told to start writing up our good people for awards because we're leaving sooner than expected and the recommendations are needed right away. I'll be glad to find better living conditions than these, but will really miss my team. We have the best crew of any admin section in the hospital. All my men are highly reliable and require almost no supervision. I genuinely like them and we try to have fun as we work, if possible.

It sounds as if some wreckage of that Chinook was found on the beach, but that's not for certain yet. It has been raining for 8 straight days now.

33 Yanks Aboard Helo Missing in Viet

By SPEC. 5 STEVE MONTIEL
S&S Staff Correspondent

SAIGON—A U.S. Army CH47 Chinook helicopter with 33 American soldiers aboard ran into bad weather Sunday afternoon and still was missing between Da Nang and Phu Bai in Vietnam Tuesday morning, the U.S. Command said.

Twenty-eight passengers from the 101st Airborne Div. and five crewmen were aboard the troop transport copter, spokesmen said.

An extensive search and rescue operation was launched immediately after contact with the helicopter was lost, the command said.

The Chinook pilot reported bad weather and declared an emergency a half-hour after the chopper left Da Nang en route to Phu Bai, according to spokesmen.

A command spokesman said rescue teams were searching ground and sea routes north of Da Nang.

Meanwhile, the U.S. Command reported Monday that three U.S. chopper crewmen were killed when an HH53 "Super Jolly Green Giant" helicopter crashed into the Nha Be River during bad weather last Thursday.

In October 1968, a CH47 helicopter crashed and killed 24 American soldiers, and a CH47 crash killed 11 South Vietnamese soldiers and injured 41 last July.

December 1971

DEC 2. "I am enclosing this clipping since I had previously mentioned the Chinook crash. It was found today, but I don't know any details yet.

Last night the girl who tends bar at our club cooked a "VC dinner" (Viet Cong) for us. It was some kind of sausage and egg roll things, plus rice, and a watery soup made with pieces of pork, potatoes, carrots, and some other roots I wasn't familiar with. It was OK, but didn't compare with steak and potatoes and hamburgers. Fortunately, I sorta expected as much and ate chicken, FF, peach pie and ice cream at the mess hall before I went. Maybe that's why it didn't taste too good to me.

Tonight, we're having a farewell party for Bill Green and one of our radio operators. They leave tomorrow. I hate to see Bill go, but I'm glad for his sake. Twelve months here.

I just realized the other day how tired I am of seeing nothing but boots and fatigues and rain suits on what few girls we have. I think I told you the nurses in Saigon wear whites. Boy, would they be out of place here, where everything is a sea of mud and water.

Everybody seems to be decorating for Christmas. The Red Cross representative at the hospital got a bunch of artificial trees and decorations, so all the wards are being adequately taken care of. It's a good thing there are a few females around, or nothing would get decorated. Most of the male officers are married, and I guess our minds are preoccupied with wives and kids. Mine is, at least."

Farewell office party for Bill Green. L-R Cpt. Burt Wilde, Cpt. James Slack, Cpt. Bill Green

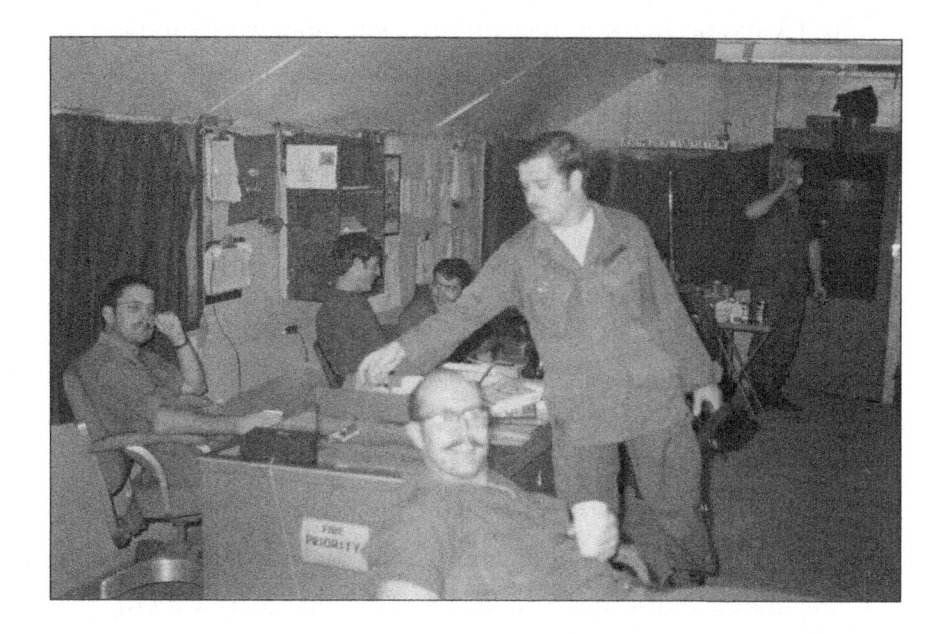

Letters Home from 85th Evacuation Hospital Vietnam, 1971

Registrar team, Back row: Cpt. Bill Green, E4 William Harper, SSG Isaac McLemore, E5 Kevin Mattingly, E3 Tom Erickstad. Sitting in front: Cpt. Burt Wilde

DEC 3. "I learned today that I will be here until the end of January and then may go to the 95th. Also, I learned that I will not get a drop with the closing of this hospital. Nine months in country is the magic number for early-out drops.

I was saddened to see Bill leave today. I didn't get to say goodbye, as I was called to a meeting when he was to leave. I sure thought a lot of him.

Burt will get a two-month drop and will be taking the 85th Evac colors (unit flag) back to the States to be retired. He's thrilled since his wife just had their second child, a girl, last week.

Today has been one of tragedies. We got more word on the Chinook this morning. It apparently hit a mountain, and all aboard were killed. A platoon of troopers was sent to secure a landing zone. We have to assume that if there were any survivors, they were either killed or captured, as the crash site was heavily booby trapped. No casualties so far from that, fortunately. It took 5 days to find it!

Then just at noon, we received a GI who had frag wounds all over, including 2 frags that entered the base of his skull and traveled to the front of his brain. It was really sad to watch him lay there and twitch and snort and roll uncomprehending eyes. We set up an urgent medivac flight to the 95th because he wasn't expected to live long since pressure was probably building in his skull. Then he started bleeding internally, so he required immediate surgery for that, and we didn't get him to Da Nang until 5:30. The saddest thing of all was that he was scheduled to go home January 13. He was on his last patrol, supposedly, and his unit was standing down in the next few days. The weather was too bad for them to be picked up by choppers, so they were walking in and set off a booby trap along the way.

Twelve straight days of rain with no break at all. Bleah!"

DEC 5. "Today all the officers were asked their preferences for their next assignments. I'm anxious to see what is done with us, as there should certainly be a flood of MSCs. I requested the 3rd Field Hospital in Saigon and the 95th in Da Nang as 1 & 2. The 67th in Quin Nhon was third."

Letters Home from 85th Evacuation Hospital Vietnam, 1971

No Survivors In Wreckage of Helo Carrying 33

S&S Vietnam Bureau

SAIGON—Searchers found no survivors Saturday in the wreckage of a CH47 Chinook helicopter that crashed last Sunday with 33 American soldiers aboard, the U.S. Command said.

The transport helicopter crashed last Sunday afternoon in rugged mountains 30 miles northwest of Da Nang near South Vietnam's northern coast.

The downed copter was spotted from the air Thursday morning, and a search patrol from the 101st Airborne Div. reached the wreckage before dusk Saturday, a command spokesman said.

Rain and low visibility hampered efforts to find the chopper and prevented search aircraft from getting close enough to the wreckage to identify it as that of the missing Chinook.

The search party slogged through rough, steep terrain and bad weather for two days before reaching the Chinook, and the men moved into a night defensive position near the crash site, a spokesman said.

The helicopter crash was the worst since 41 American troops were killed in a CH53 copter crash in Jan. 1968.

The Chinook was carrying 28 passengers and five crewmen from Da Nang to Phu Bai when it went down in bad weather. All the men were from the 101st

DEC 7. "There seems to be a high rate of loss for cassettes sent from Nam. I guess since blanks are so hard to get, they are a popular item among postal workers. The ones sent this direction usually get here all right. Also, thanks again for the *Sports Illustrated* (recent copies), as they are very rare this far north and greatly appreciated.

I called to check on our R&R and was told we didn't get it. I immediately requested Feb 1, but was told we might not get that either. I'm depressed. The problem is that so many are getting their drops and are moving up their R&R requests. Also, the Army seems to be decreasing drastically the number of flights. The whole country seems to be in mass confusion with all the troop withdrawals. It's hard to catch a flight anywhere in-country now since so many of us are being shuffled around.

The kid with leukemia I mentioned that Mike Miller was going to send to Saigon was discharged today. He was weakening rapidly, and I guess Mike decided he was now beyond help. His parents got a ride down here today, and Mike decided to let them take him home since they might not be able to get back down before he died. It's very sad, but unfortunately just a common occurrence in the struggle for survival among these poor country peasants.

About 4:00 a.m. we received 6 U.S. casualties, all with MFW (multiple fragmentation wounds). One was critically injured and was flown on to Da Nang before daylight. They were caught in a mortar attack which may have been from friendly forces."

DEC 8. "Don't bother to send me a Houston paper. Mom had the Lufkin paper sent and it's always 2–3 weeks late, and I don't know many of the people or events happening, so don't get much from it. The *Stars and Stripes* is very comprehensive plus having a lot of war news, so I stay pretty well informed. Thanks, though.

The WWII military currency you sent is much like the money we use here, except that ours is in dollars. It is in varying sizes also, according to denomination. No one is allowed to have real U.S. money over here."

DEC 9. "Today has been the most interesting I have spent in Nam. The CO of the 67th Medical Group wanted to see Hue, so our XO set up an ARVN NCO [Army of the Republic of Vietnam Non-Commissioned Officer] to guide, and the touring group grew until there were about 25 of us along with our cameras. We left at 10:30 and didn't return until 5:00.

We started by taking several cases of baby food to the ARVN hospital and then toured it. Their situation is very sad. They have 1,150 beds and very little and very outdated equipment. They have only a few poorly trained doctors, and the wards are all open-air, French-built masonry buildings. The wards smelled much like a zoo, as the sheets are not changed very often. Chickens, ducks, dogs, rats, and flies seemed to abound. Now I can appreciate how easily the ARVNs accept death. They have so little to work with and so many to work on, they can't begin to do much for any.

Next, we had lunch at a restaurant. I had a watery crab-asparagus soup and then some thinly sliced abalone in a broth of vegetables unknown to me. We were only given chopsticks with which to eat, although we got spoons for the soup. I managed to feed myself, but wouldn't exactly pass for a native. Our drink was a native beer.

Next, we went by Hue University and then on to the Citadel. That is the old walled fortress which included the emperor's palace and harem quarters. Most of it has been looted, but enough is left inside that we could tell it was fantastically royal and elegant 100s of years ago. This was the part of Hue where a lot of the Tet Offensive battle in '68 was fought. Everywhere there were bullet marks and holes blasted in walls and a few collapsed buildings. Even in downtown Hue, most buildings are still shot up. It reminded me of the tower at UT after the Whitman shootings. This major battle was fought at Hue because it is essentially the second capital of South Vietnam, and its fall would have been a great victory for the communists. I took lots of pictures.

Next, we went far out into the country to an ancient tomb and gardens of a king (Chinese, I believe). Our interpreter either didn't know or couldn't express himself well enough to give us much information. It was interesting to get out and see how the peasants live, growing rice and herding buffalo and cattle and grubbing roots, living in thatched roofed little huts. I don't care to make a habit of going out like that, though.

Driving back through the slum area of the city (all housing looked like slums), some kids threw a dead snake (don't know what kind) into the back of our truck. Then a "cowboy" (teen boys who run up and try to grab watches, cameras, etc.) jumped on the tailgate as the truck slowed down and appeared about to grab for my watch just as I was about to kick him back, and suddenly he jumped off again with no harm done to either side."

The truck we were in was a "deuce and a half," the standard ten-wheeled main truck the Army has used for decades. I mention it here because it was a serious source of finger amputations. When men jumped out the back of them, frequently their rings would snag on the tailgates, and the weight of the individual would just yank his ring finger off.

"Still no word on where I'll go next. All officers except MSCs now know."

DEC 10. "I spent most of the day writing award recommendations and citations for my men in preparation for our closing. I am recommending Sgt. McLemore for a bronze star and two of my radio operators for the Army Commendation Medal. For all the others I am writing letters of appreciation to be put in their personnel records. Most of my men have not been here long enough for medals, but they are certainly outstanding men.

I checked on my request for a drop for school today and learned it was forwarded to Long Binh two weeks ago, so I wonder if it might go through yet.

I may look into a charter flight/reduced fare deal for wives to Bangkok. The R&R situation projects to get even worse, so maybe we could meet in Thailand."

DEC 11. "Looks like Christmas here won't be too hot for sure, as many of my friends will be gone by then. A lot of the doctors and nurses are beginning to leave already. Looks like I may be staying and that doesn't thrill me at all, although that's not definite yet.

We learned that Bob Hope won't be stopping here this year because we don't have 35 BCs. That's a bum deal! What about the guys who have hepatitis and malaria, etc.? They're still bedridden. He will be coming to Camp Eagle, so I hope to see him there. Evidently, many over here think he has lost touch with what's going on.

You probably heard about the letter 50 doctors in Long Binh and Saigon wrote to the Senate (copy enclosed). It infuriates a lot of us here, as we can just imagine the kind of doctors who signed it, as we have a bunch here. They are draftees who buck the system constantly, creating morale problems, possibly slighting patient care in the process. Those guys need to get out in the sticks for a while and see a few battle casualties. As Bill Green said, "They have all the luxuries and nothing to do but bitch." They might be right in a lot of ways, but I'm afraid what they've done will be sensationalized and taken out of proportion.

To top it all off, a request (order) was sent out for statistics from the Surgeon General today. We were given about four hours to work up a bunch of statistics that I feel are practically meaningless without some qualifying statements to explain that they are not complete and not much weight should be placed on them. With the short fuse we were given, I had to put almost my whole staff to digging through records to find out how many patients were admitted since July with self-inflicted wounds and how many from fights. I'll bet a million dollars will be spent researching and rebutting what those docs said.

Last night a 1st Lt. died in the ER that no one has the vaguest idea from what. He was found in his hooch gasping for breath with bleeding from his mouth and his jaws clamped shut. We requested an autopsy. That should be very interesting.

Dear Janie

50 Army Doctors in Viet Urge Pullout

WASHINGTON (UPI) —Fifty U.S. Army doctors in Vietnam said Wednesday that most of the U.S. casualties they treat result from self-inflicted wounds, fighting among GIs, auto accidents, jungle diseases and drugs —and not from combat.

A U.S. command spokesman in Saigon declined to comment on the report.

The report — in the form of a letter addressed to "Senators of the United States" —was read to the Senate by Democratic Leader Mike Mansfield, who said, "I am shocked by what I have read."

He said the letter was signed by 50 officers in the Army Medical Corps who work at two of the biggest U.S. hospitals in Vietnam —the 3rd Field Hospital in Saigon and the 24th Evacuation Hospital in Long Binh, a Saigon suburb.

The doctors appealed for an immediate and total withdrawal of U.S. forces from Vietnam.

"We see little good coming from our endeavors to our servicemen, to our allies or to the Vietnamese" who "strongly feel the fighting and dying they know so well will end when the American forces leave this country and that our presence tends only to prolong their suffering."

The doctors wrote:

"The majority of the medical problems are presently of three kinds: (1) traumatic mostly due to automobile accidents, self-inflicted wounds or wounds sustained by in-fighting amongst our own troops; (2)

(Continued on Back Page, Col. 2)

Also, we received a VC with both legs blown off. His two comrades were killed. They were couriers between Hue and their unit, and our intelligence guys got a lot of info from him.

I flew down to Da Nang on a spur of the moment deal today. I was able to take care of my investigation, but the flight was such a hurry-up thing I didn't have time to grab my camera. I could have gotten some great pictures. The flight covers a good cross section of VN since it covers coastal lowlands, rice paddies, foothills, mountains, bays, and the city of Da Nang itself. The mountains are quite beautiful, although also quite ominous as they are laced with waterfalls cascading hundreds of feet down their sides. We were only there for about an hour, which was just enough time to do what I needed and get back before the weather closed in."

I didn't write home about the rest of the story on that short trip. Our Huey got hit somewhere over Da Nang, so we figured it might have been from some doped-up GI. I always wondered if those red crosses on dustoffs weren't inviting targets, anyway. When we landed back at the 85th, we all climbed out to check for damage and found that the spotlight under the main body had been hit. I was walking toward the back under the tail boom, inspecting it, when the crew chief came around the front and screamed at me to stop. The rear rotor was still spinning, but was totally silent and I had not noticed that I was about to walk into it. To this day, that memory gives me the shivers.

There were also other events that occurred I didn't write Janie about. One day, an ARVN was brought in that had been hit in the back by an RPG (rocket-propelled grenade). The grenade didn't explode and pierced the victim's body and lodged in his scrotum. Five or six of us all gathered around to hold the ARVN still so that he wouldn't trigger the grenade while the doctor determined his treatment approach. Next, in a very amazing act of bravery, the doctor asked for one medic volunteer to stay to assist him and told everyone else to exit the ER immediately. These two were able to extract the grenade without exploding it. I always felt those men should have been awarded a medal for bravery, but I never heard if that happened.

Another event occurred late one night when I was AOD. I was patrolling the compound and walked into the ER. Our NCOD (NCO of the day) was looking for me and told me a group of high black soldiers were holed up in the EM housing area and had announced they would kill any "honkey" that intruded on them. He told me he was not about to go down there. I guess I felt a quick decision had to be made because some clueless white guy might stumble into some real trouble. We always wore our .45 pistols when on duty but were prohibited from putting a clip in them unless threatened. That night I loaded mine, took a deep breath, and headed down to the enlisted quarters. I never found the party but must admit I didn't look very hard, either. I figured if they were shooting heroin, they would probably nod off pretty fast, and maybe that's what happened. I feel sure I wrote up a report on it, but don't recall any further action taken or questions asked about the incident.

Another rainy night when I was AOD, I walked into the ER to find a very agitated group of four soldiers who were demanding to see a friend who had been brought to the 85th. They had circled my small A&D clerk and seemed ready to do him harm for refusing their request. When I demanded to know what was going on, they turned on me and said, "And just who the hell are you?" I was wearing a poncho, so quickly pulled my collar out from under the hood so they could see my captain bars. I told them I was Captain Slack and was in charge of the hospital at that moment, and they really needed to calm down or some MPs would be escorting them out the gate. Fortunately, they realized the error of their ways, and I suggested they come back the next day during business hours as I pointed them to the door.

The experiences of working in a hospital heightened our awareness of how dangerous it was just to exist in a war zone. One day, we got a Soldier in who had been shot in the lower arm while just riding in a jeep. It was interesting because he never heard the shot or saw the shooter. Curiously, it was a .38 caliber bullet that was extracted, which means it was from a revolver, a weapon we seldom saw.

We also saw numerous snakebites, a few drownings, some electrocutions (primarily from guys trying to erect TV antennas on roofs that had hot wires close by), not to mention the fraggings (deliberate attempts to kill an unpopular senior officer, usually with a hand grenade) and fights to be expected with so much testosterone from men trained to fight and with access to lots of weapons.

DEC 12. "I got another letter from my cousin Sandra today. Actually, all my relatives have written me quite well. Certainly, much better than I would have thought or hoped for.

I was off today and played a little basketball with one of the dustoff crews. Afterwards, they had to run a check flight and asked if I wanted to go up and take pictures, so I jumped at the chance. I took about 30 shots, but didn't get all I wanted of Hue since we got called back on a mission. It was to take a GI who had burned his eyes in the mess hall down to Da Nang. So, I got some pictures of Da Nang after all. 20 slides."

Apparently, all my slides got accidentally thrown away in one of our moves. We don't have a single one.

DEC 13. I'm so fed up with this whole situation—all the skag freaks, loud mouthed mal-contents, and our XO. He showed me my efficiency report today. He rated me an 80, which I took as a personal slap since I got a 96 and a 97 at Ft. Gordon. I've only recently begun to get confidence in myself in my new job, but I've always been conscientious in my efforts. Certainly, I've heard no other complaints from the staff and it really galls me that this one guy should rate me so low. I think I am the only MSC at the hospital not recommended for some meritorious award. I hashed it out with this guy for quite a while, but evidently, I should have stomped and cussed. It's sure hard not to get a "screw it" attitude sometimes."

DEC 14. "It looks like now that I may be staying here. A smaller dispensary type outfit will be moving in. It will be staffed by two internists, two surgeons, a nurse anesthetist and some medics. I'm being considered to stay and help as an administrator. That should be better than being a drug counselor at one of the rehab centers, although I had hoped to improve my living conditions. I am trying to swing a job with one of the dustoff units as an admin officer in Da Nang, but not much hope of that.

Today a dustoff pilot named Don Slack walked into the mess hall. He flies out of Qui Nhon (pronounced kwee-nyawn) and we both agreed that neither of us had actually met another Slack. He is from California, so we're probably not related."

DEC 15. "My day was taken up entertaining an LTC Seely. He is chief of all Registrars in Nam and he came up to see our operation and check on our stand down procedures. He had no complaints and seemed well satisfied with all we were doing. Bill deserves most of that credit, no doubt. Our shop is generally regarded as the smoothest in VN evidently. The LTC told me there were no more registrars' slots open in VN, but he would mention me for a dustoff admin job since I preferred that to being in a drug center. I told him what I wanted most was a drop and showed him Shannon's pictures, etc., but there's nothing he can do about that.

An ARVN general sent one of his staff down today to arrange a Christmas stand-down ceremony here. We had hoped to have the hospital cleared by the 25th, but he wants us to have 50 patients so he can bring 40 girls and TV cameras to present all the patients gifts and selected staff members with medals. It would be a grave social error not to honor his request, but a great pain in the neck to try to evacuate that many patients by January 1. I came up with the idea to fill our beds with ARVNs and then move them to Hue ARVN hospital the next day. That would also impress the VN people watching TV. Our XO thought that was a brilliant idea, so that helped my damaged ego somewhat.

We received 2 GIs with frag wounds today, the first in several days. We also got in an ARVN that was pretty well messed up. All from booby traps."

DEC 17. "Last night I got a call after I went to bed that Camp Eagle and Camp Evans (just the other side of Hue, Eagle is on this side) were under ground attack. I dressed and rushed over to the ER. Both our dustoffs were already airborne, and several gunships had scrambled. We finally made contact with Eagle and Evans, and they said all was quiet. It was all a false alarm, and I learned today that even Da Nang was supposed to have been hit. We all traced our radio calls and pieced it together, and apparently some GI in Da Nang had gotten on a radio and started calling. We're still not certain what happened, but it sure broke the monotony. Naturally there were some raging pilots since it is so extremely dangerous to fly at night.

This afternoon I got a message to call our personnel office in Da Nang. They said that my request for early out had never reached Long Binh. It had left Da Nang on Nov 24. They suggested I type it up and send it again, but that it still needed to go to Washington. I have been fuming all night and have already written the Col. in Washington I wrote before. I think I will call Long Binh tomorrow and try to talk to the top man there, whoever he is. I imagine that request is still sitting on someone's desk and I certainly intend to find it or raise hell looking for it."

DEC 18. "I talked to Maj. Jones, who is our XO as well as Inspector General for the hospital, about my drop papers being lost. He investigated, and sure enough, they were lost and I would have to resubmit them. Naturally our hospital HQ (his office) had lost their copy of the request, too. Fortunately, I had made sure I had copies of all of it. I had my own man retype the request, and since Maj. Jones is going to Long Binh tomorrow, he is going to carry it to 67th Medical group himself to speed it up. I also wrote the Col. in Washington and told him what had happened. The apathy and inefficiency over here are incredible."

I enclosed a copy of my correspondence to the Surgeon General's office in D.C. It is evidence of a life lesson I learned: "If you don't ask, the answer will always be no."

"We had two deaths today. One was a VN woman who drank some Parathion insecticide in order to kill herself. It took two days, but finally did the job.

Dear Janie

DEPARTMENT OF THE ARMY
85th EVACUATION HOSPITAL (SMBL)
APO SAN FRANCISCO 96308

AVBJ-CC-SC-R   18 DECEMBER 1971

COL. E.R. MCCANDLESS
CHIEF, PERSONNEL & TRAINING DIVISION
OFFICE OF THE SURGEON GENERAL
DEPARTMENT OF THE ARMY
WASHINGTON, D.C. 20315

Dear Sir:

I recently sent you a request for early release from active duty in order to attend school. I stated in the letter that the original copy of the request was being forwarded through channels, and asked your assistance in expediting the processing of it.

Today I learned that the request was sent out by 67th Mediacl Group on 24 November 1971, but has not reached USA MEDCOMV. I have initiated another request which will be hand carried through to USA MEDCOMV tomorrow. Approval has been recommended by this HQ and by HQ, 67th Medical Group, and since the 85th Evac Hospital is presently standing down, no replacement will be necessary for my slot as Registrar.

I do not think this second request can be completely processed in time for the start of the spring semester, should it be approved. Therefore, I must again ask your assistance in expediting this matter if it is within your power. Your help will be greatly appreciated.

Sincerely Yours,

JAMES G. SLACK
CPT   MSC

Late this evening, a U.S. intelligence officer called and requested permission to bring an NVA prisoner to our hospital. When the ARVNs capture a wounded prisoner, they are supposed to take them to their own hospital. This one was in bad shape and stood a much better chance of being saved by our staff, so was brought here. He was shot in the chest, jaw, and both legs. He died about 10 minutes later in the ER.

We've had a VC in the hospital for a week now and he told one of our nurses that he was 18 and that the Viet Cong had come to his village and threatened to kill his family if he didn't fight with them. It's like a bad dream to realize how cruel and unscrupulous the enemy is and how senseless this all is when the communists must rely on such tactics to gain soldiers."

DEC 19. "I guess that by the time you get this, Christmas '71 will already be gone. The thought of missing Shannon's first Christmas of really being aware is extremely painful.

One of my men got a terrible "Dear John" letter last week. His girl said she wouldn't wait for him and she was now very serious about another boy. Can you believe that? My guy has held up very well as far as I can tell. Just knowing that someone back there loves you and is waiting for your return is a tremendous morale booster, probably more than girls know. Something as bad as that must have just the opposite effect. No doubt it's hard on the girls, too, especially if the flame goes out, to write often. But boy, is that girl's name mud around here!"

DEC 20. "We got in six U.S. booby trap victims today. Four of them required surgery, so we sent three of them to the 95th and operated on the other one. We only have one OR left since the other two have been converted to a lab in preparation for the dispensary moving into the hospital proper. The ER crew also brought a dead ARVN back to life. That is always exciting, but his survival is doubtful. He was badly torn up by shrapnel."

DEC 21. "The ARVN we revived yesterday died this afternoon. He used 70 units of blood and was still bleeding. His nurse asked me if they had to remove his bandages before his body was sent to the morgue because that was about all that was holding his legs to his body."

DEC 22. "I learned today that I will be reassigned to the 68th Medical Group. About all that means is that I will be in the southern half of Nam. Presently, I'm with the 67th Medical Group which runs the medical outfits in the northern half.

Farrah Fawcett's picture (pin-up in bathing suit) was in an Army magazine we got today. Knew you would be thrilled to know that little bit of info."

I guess it should be mentioned here that Farrah was a next-door neighbor in my apartment building the summer of my senior year at UT. But Janie and I were dating, so I never gave her a second look (yeah, right) and vice versa.

DEC 24. "Today started with a "stand down appreciation" ceremony, presided over by the Commanding General of the First ARVN Division. There was a troop formation and 50 VN high school girls presenting gifts to patients. Naturally there were all kinds of U.S. brass there, too.

Then at 12:15 we loaded into trucks and went to Camp Eagle to see the Bob Hope show. There was bright sunshine all day for the first time in a month, and we all got burned. The show lasted two hours and was good, but naturally not as polished as it is on TV. If some of the show is televised, I was back at the far-left corner of a section of patients. They are all in pale blue PJs.

Maybe I've been here too long, but some of the girls were unbelievably beautiful. All in all, it was pretty good, but some of his jokes seemed irrelevant to me. Many were about ecology in the U.S. and they seemed out of place when we're over here bombing and killing and polluting like crazy. Oh, yes, two of the girls were from Texas and flashed "hook 'em" several times. That sure looked good to me.

I really got angry because the trucks left early, and I didn't have time to grab my camera. I was sick about that but had to run to catch a truck. Burt Wilde got left and missed the show.

When we sang "Silent Night" at the end, it gave me chills, even though it was 90 degrees and sunny. Next year, we'll be together and that's a promise. I love you. Merry Christmas."

Dear Janie

Stars & Stripes Dec 27, 1971

Hope Brings Sunshine to Camp Eagle GIs

By SPEC. 4 MARK TREADUP
S&S Staff Correspondent

CAMP EAGLE, Vietnam — Bob Hope didn't really change the recent spell of bad weather in the northern part of South Vietnam, but he did bring a lot of sunshine to an estimated 8,500 GIs at this big American base near Hue on Christmas Eve.

Hope's first Vietnam performance with his current Christmas troupe started in pouring rain at Da Nang Tuesday, and a show planned for Wednesday on the USS Coral Sea was canceled because of poor weather.

However, Hope's first cue card was the only thing canceled Friday at Camp Eagle. The prepared card had read: "How hard does it have to rain before they end this war?"

The afternoon sun shined brightly throughout the performances of Hope, Jim Nabors, Les Brown and his Band of Renown, Suzanne Charney, Jan Daley, the Blue Streaks, Sunday's Child, the Hollywood Deb Stars, and Brucene Smith, Miss World U.S.A.

The show started shortly after 1 p.m. with Les Brown's band playing "Jesus Christ Superstar." Hope, carrying a golf club, made his ad-libbing entrance on stage soon after that.

"Oh, I love it," he said pointing to a sign in the audience, "Bob Hope for vice-president."

"I never hit anyone with a golf ball in my life," he quipped.

"San Mateo," he said pointing at another placard. "Boy did that guy ever take a wrong turn."

Hope got a big hand from the GIs when he asked, "where were you guys hiding when the withdrawal took place."

"This is where it's at," he said, "just a few minutes by rocket from everyplace."

Hope's biting humor hit at mosquitos, monsoon mud, pollution, population and the California earthquake.

Hope stood back to listen and watch as Suzanne Charny sang and danced through "Don't Tell Mama," and then brought out the Oakland Athletics' star pitcher, Vida Blue.

Part way through their dialogue and before their duet Blue Stars was kissed by a GI from her home state, and four soldiers got to dance with the three girls of Sunday's Child.

Hope got a rise out of the Army audience when he complained that as a baseball player he was "just a piece of property."

"They can move you wherever they want,'' he said.

"I'm not sure I understand,'' said Hope, "but I guess these guys know what you're talking about."

Jan Daley, a beautiful blonde, sang the "Theme from Love Story," with one arm around a lucky GI from the audience. Each of the 10 Hollywood Deb Stars was kissed by a GI from her home state, and four soldiers got to dance with the three girls of Sunday's Child.

Jim Nabors, dressed in a red shirt, red-white-and-blue slacks and white shoes, brought the crowd to its feet in a standing ovation when he finished singing "The Impossible Dream."

At the conclusion of the show Jan Daley led the cast and servicemen in singing "Silent Night." It was Christmas eve afternoon, and not all the singers were dry-eyed.

Hope said after the show, "I was thrilled to see some empty seats."

He said he played before 28,000 in Da Nang last year and only 12,500 this year, but he wasn't bothered by the falling attendance.

"It'd be nice to come back here to play to an empty house some time," he said.

DEC 25. "We had a floor show last night with free drinks, then a mail call at midnight. I was thrilled to get the card of the 17th and your letters of the 18th and 19th. I wrote you back at 1:30 a.m.

My men woke me up at 3:30 a.m. to get me to come out and drink some more with them, but I couldn't and wouldn't. Then I had to go to the office at 9:30 a.m. and set up an evacuation for 12 patients. A clerk usually does that, but he didn't make it in.

We had the basic turkey dinner for lunch, which means leftovers tonight. The floor show was Korean and very good. Everyone was in the spirit, and we all had a pretty good time. Your letters coming at midnight finished it all off on a great note.

Also, all of us got sacks of various little gifts from church and military wives groups. I got a nice leather wallet and a key ring. We got piles of homemade Christmas cards from several sororities, too. It's good to know that so many people still put forth the effort for those of us still left here.

I was in the ER a while ago and there was a drunk all strapped down and threatening to kill everyone. The doctor told the MPs to take him to jail, as he was only drunk. He calmed down and promised to behave, so they didn't cuff him. He immediately spit in the face of one of the MPs and then kicked him in the lower stomach. The other MPs grabbed him, and the Sgt. who runs X-Ray slugged the guy. They cuffed him and threw him to the floor of a jeep and hauled him off. He'll probably get worked over a little more at the jail. The MP was taken back to the ER in severe pain but proved to be OK. We X-Rayed the Sgt.'s hand, but nothing was broken.

The drunk said he had been run off by his parents at 13. I thought, *What a sad case he is, with no friends and threatening to kill people on Christmas."*

DEC 26. "The leaflets were dropped Dec. 24 and hundreds fluttered down during the Bob Hope show. These are explaining about the new white dustoff choppers and that they shouldn't be shot at. Occasionally, we see leaflets urging the VC and NVA to defect, also.

We got another suicide today. A GI shot himself, but I didn't learn any details. That's the first one we've received in a good while. I don't know why they tapered off like that."

DEC 27. "I am now in bed with some sort of bug. Nausea, chills, aches, diarrhea. Flu is going around here, so maybe that's what I have. The good weather left with Christmas, and it is overcast and blowing a damp chill from the ocean now.

My new hooch is away from the runway and among other hooches now. Several of our folks ran to the bunkers

Christmas night because there was so much artillery firing. Our gunners must have been counting down to the end of the truce because I've never heard so much pounding as I did that night."

DEC 28. "Our five wards have all been emptied of patients and equipment now. We still have 6 patients in ICU. It will be the only ward open when the 85th becomes a dispensary. I finally got orders transferring me to the 68th Group for reassignment. That still doesn't tell me very much. Most of the doctors and nurses leave in the next 2 or 3 days I suppose.

I'm sorry you got upset on the phone today, Honey. I'm sure I don't fully realize how rough this is on you. I should be leaving VN exactly four months from today, so I guess this is the halfway point. That should be encouraging, but it seems like a long time still."

DEC 30. "The movie tonight was *Getting Straight* with Elliott Gould and Candice Bergen. It was better than I expected, but still had all the protest scenes, etc. that bugged me.

We had a big party for the whole staff of the 85th this afternoon.

I called Long Binh today to find out where I go next, but they had never heard of me and had no idea what to do with me. They are getting 5 to 10 MSCs every two weeks and are frantic to find jobs for them, so here's hoping."

DEC 31. "I got bumped on the roster and ended up on AOD tonight. All of us in Registrar put in $3 apiece to buy food and booze for a New Year's Eve party, so I'm really hacked. I won't be partying since we are on alert and I must spend most of my time in the orderly room. I will also be spending the night here, awake if possible. There are parties going on everywhere, not to mention Registrar's.

Tonight, at midnight the 85th is officially deactivated, although it still lacks a lot of work yet. I've really been amazed at how disorganized the whole thing has become. The top brass has changed its mind three times about who and what will take over medical responsibilities. Our hospital CO seems to have little feel or no interest in what's going on and has given me absolutely no guidance about what to do. He has not even asked any questions about what I'm doing. He has been in the registrar shop once and the XO twice since I've been here, so it's surprising they can judge the job I do at all, much less rate me poorly. I'm now making every decision I can concerning patient dispositions and policies to be used by the new units. How many times I've wished junior officers could rate their seniors!

I still must say that except for the leadership, I have enjoyed my job and my coworkers here. All the rest of the nurses and most of the doctors leave tomorrow."

4,370 Spaces Cut

SAIGON (S&S) — Twenty-six U.S. Army units, including the 85th Evac. Hospital at Phu Bai and the 307th Air Traffic Control Bn. at Bien Hoa, began stand down New Year's Day, the U.S. command said. Redeployment of the units will involve about 4,370 spaces, spokesmen said.

January 1972

JAN 1, 1972. "I finally got to bed at 8:00 a.m. and slept until 2:00 p.m. Last night's celebration was really something and a little frightening. Flares and smoke grenades were going off all around us, not to mention a few machine guns. Tracer bullets were going up everywhere and about 12:10 a.m. we heard a loud explosion across the road at an engineering unit. It turned out to be some explosive device that had been set off under an NCO's hooch. I heard it was destroyed, but no one was hurt. The rest of the night was quiet after that.

Most of our people have left now, and I guess that's a part of the empty, futile feeling I have tonight."

JAN 2. "I have been surprisingly busy today, especially for a Sunday. I have been making up the final bills on civilian U.S. contractors seen in December and getting ready for the final audit of my books tomorrow.

This morning another of those endless tragic cases occurred. A young captain was brought in by a slick. He had been shot through his thigh by a .51 cal. Chinese machine gun. He had bled out, and I knew he was dead as soon as I saw him, although we did chest compressions for a while anyway. He had been flying one of the unarmed Low Observation Helicopters (Loach) that the NVA have been downing a lot of over in the A Shau Valley a few miles west of us. He might have survived if the gunship crew that picked him up had realized how serious he was or been better at stopping blood loss.

The sad part was that today was his last day to fly and he was to leave tomorrow for the U.S. The Army was rifting him (Reduction In Force, releasing him due to an excess of pilots)."

I vividly remember this case, because it was the final death I saw in Vietnam. Most of our remaining personnel were at a farewell floor show. That was unusual because it was in the afternoon, was at the EM club, and officers were included. Suddenly, word spread that a dustoff was coming in hot, and the ER team took off on the run.

"Incidentally, the captain shot through the thigh took over his job (scout platoon leader) from a Cpt. Burchfield who was also shot and died here over a month ago.

The husband of one of our nurses also had a similar assignment, and the Army is rifting him, too. His unit called him to fly a mission last week, and he told them "Hell no." He leaves for home this week."

JAN 3. "I spent the day with Ron Hudak, an MSC captain who is Asst. Registrar at the 95th Evac. He will be custodian of all the records of the 85th. We send all records from the previous year down there so that if any problems arise the records will still be in Nam and easy to check on. Ron just came up from being Registrar at the Cam Ranh Bay Drug Treatment Center. He is a West Point graduate and got into MSCs because his physical profile kept him out of the infantry. Very lucky!

We have our official stand down ceremony tomorrow, and I hope to have my section completely closed out in the next day or so. Sgt. McLemore left yesterday on leave and three of my men leave in three days, so things are rapidly drawing to a close.

I'm now reading H.G. Wells' *The Time Machine* and *War of the Worlds*. Both were childhood favorites of mine (probably in the form of classic comic books)."

JAN 4. "No mail again today, and I am a little depressed tonight. The new people have taken over the hospital facilities, and the mess hall is now filled with strangers, as are most of the hooches. It really seems strange to see all these unfamiliar faces instead of all the old friends that have worked together and been so close.

Two separate units have moved in and will work together. They are 1st Platoon, 616th Medical Company and B Co.,

326 Medical Battalion, so now we know! There will be as many people here as ever, but only about 6 or 7 doctors and no nurses, only medics. There will be one ward with about 20 beds, with a holding capacity of 72 hours. Any longer than that and the patient should be evaced to the 95th. Many of the new guys comprise Eagle Dustoff. It has about 6 or 7 choppers, and they are responsible for picking up 101st patients, while Phu Bai Dustoff picks up ARVNs and all other U.S. personnel. It will still keep two ships here.

We had our official stand down ceremony today. It started to rain, so it was shortened and conducted in the EM club instead of at the helipad. It was sort of touching actually to realize that this hospital was closing after all the men and suffering and death it has seen. It's been in VN since 1965 and in Phu Bai since 1969.

While we were all on the pad before it began to rain, the dustoff crew scrambled, and it really touched us all. We have seen that so many times, and it always put the wheels in frenzied motion. This time, they brought back a chopper pilot who had been shot through the leg by a .50 cal. bullet. He was with the same unit as the Cpt. who died two days ago and was flying the same kind of chopper in the same area, the A Shau. It really tore a hole in him, but fortunately did not hit his femoral artery as happened with the other Cpt. He will be OK—at least he will live.

The XO did deliver my request to Long Binh, but I don't expect much to come of it. Still, it doesn't hurt to be prepared. I am primarily concerned about vet school, though."

JAN 5. "We've been trying to get all our reports and loose ends tied off so we can close Registrar. McLemore went on leave, and Burt has been in Da Nang for four days, so I've been running around like mad. I hope to get all our furnishings and equipment turned in tomorrow morning and then go down to the 95th tomorrow afternoon to take all our records and sign over a couple of funds I'm responsible for. I should stay there overnight.

On top of that, I've been trying to help the two men being left as A&D clerks for the dispensary get squared away. An officer should have been sent up to explain what should be done. What mass confusion!

I met another Slack today! This time it was a colored Sgt. from Tacoma, Wash. I can't get over meeting two Slacks within 3 weeks."

JAN 6. "I'm now in beautiful Da Nang at the 95th Evac and am not in any rush to get back. I'd forgotten what a desolate hole Phu Bai was. The Registrar here has his own jeep (we had to catch rides the best way we could), so tonight we loaded up and went to the Tien Sha Naval Support Base Officers Club for dinner. It was as nice as many of the better restaurants in the U.S. We got to pick out our own steaks from a selection of 1" rib eyes or 2" New York strips. We also had rolls, brussels sprouts, baked potatoes, salad, soup, onion rings, and ice cream. We ate by candlelight and had a movie to watch while we ate, or an American floor show in the next room. And when I got back, I got to take a hot shower and stay in as long as I wanted—and it was even in the same building as my quarters! I have to watch myself or I will run it into the ground about how good these people have it and don't realize it.

Registrar at the 85th is now nonexistent. We cleared out all the office furniture today, and the building is bare. I hope I get my new assignment soon, as I have very little to do there and no base of operations anymore. Time will really drag, and I'm anxious to get into a new job and make new friends."

JAN 7. "I am still in Da Nang since I didn't finish all I needed to do today. I hope to catch a chopper back tomorrow, and in a way, it will be good to get back to my little home away from home. Here, I am staying in a Cpt.'s room who is on R&R. The quarters are in three two-story buildings with rooms back-to-back, motel style. There are bathrooms in the middle of both floors.

The Registrar crew went back to the Naval base to play basketball after chow, but I passed as I've caught some crud. They also have a tennis court here at the 95th.

Letters Home from 85th Evacuation Hospital Vietnam, 1971

The main reason I don't feel so hot is that our R&R didn't go through for February, either. I immediately put in for March. I was #14 and seven were granted."

JAN 8. "I'm back in Phu Bai again. I was able to catch a ride on a dustoff this afternoon after about giving up on finding a ride. The weather has been very bad for the past three days and not much is flying. This one was making an instrument flight for training and was therefore on radar. It was actually safer than normal flights, I imagine, as we were at 10,000 feet and high above the clouds, other traffic, mountains, and gunfire.

The 1st Lt. who will be the Admin. Officer for the 616th here came up with me. What a dufus! He's the "gung-ho, look for action" type and wants to get out of the MSCs and into the MPs. When I told him it was safer to fly to Phu Bai, he said he would rather go by convoy and maybe get a Purple Heart. His deck is definitely missing some cards.

I just wish I would find out my next assignment and go on to it so I could make some definite plans. Mainly, I just want the hell out of this whole damn country and back to my family."

JAN 9. "I finally made myself accept that my drop for school is not going to come through. I must admit I really thought it would since the XO took it to Long Binh that second time. They sent it to Washington right away on the 4th, and

I checked yesterday and they still hadn't heard anything. At least I tried not to give you reason for optimism, even though I was excited about it. I had intended to come home and surprise you!

I will send in my application for vet school tomorrow. Also, I've decided to go ahead and pack up and go down to Long Binh and hurry a new assignment out of them. This waiting with nothing to do and constant bad weather is getting on my nerves."

JAN 10. "I intend to start clearing tomorrow and hopefully be down to Long Binh by the weekend. I suppose you might as well continue to send mail to this address, and it will be forwarded. I'll call you when I get a new address.

I flew down to Da Nang and back again this afternoon. I had some more records to turn into the 95th and some radio equipment for the 571st Dustoff Detachment. I'm still trying to finagle a job there. I really like those pilots, and they seem anxious for me to get assigned there."

Homecoming

January 10, 1972 was the last letter I sent home from Vietnam. What follows are my memories of the whirlwind of events that ensued in the next few days.

On January 11, I got a call from Burt Wilde who I believe was preparing to board a helicopter that would begin his journey home with the flag of the 85th (to Ft. Campbell, KY, if my memory serves). He saw my name somewhere on a list of approved drops and called me with the news. He also told me a chopper was leaving for Da Nang in about two hours, and he would try to hold a spot on it for me. I don't remember what all happened in that short time, other than me throwing what few things I owned in a suitcase Janie's folks had sent me for Christmas, bidding a few farewells, and racing towards that chopper.

I landed at the Da Nang air base which included the out-processing center for those leaving Nam. I was then assigned a bunk in a huge barracks and instructed to check twice a day for my name on the latest flight manifests. That was a popular spot! I had no opportunity to call home and alert my family. I think it was two days before my name appeared for a flight leaving at dawn the next morning. After chow that evening, we were confined to an open-air pen of hurricane fencing and locked in. It had a tin roof and several picnic tables to sit on but was very much open to the chilly ocean breeze

Dear Janie

that blew all night. We had all exchanged our fatigues and boots for our short-sleeved khaki uniforms, and none of us had jackets, but we didn't complain. Dog handlers and their German Shepherds patrolled the perimeter all night. In the early hours before dawn, we were lined up single file and had to open our trousers and submit to a pat down search. The intent was to be sure we were not smuggling weapons, souvenirs, porn, or drugs. Once we got our pants pulled up, we were lined up and prepared to board a Flying Tiger DC-8 commercial airliner. I will always remember sitting on the tarmac and watching a flight of four F-4 Phantoms take off in a group with a tremendous roar and orange fire shooting from their engines in the early twilight. I was really glad they were on our team!

As one might imagine, there was a concerted roar of elation as we lifted off the ground, and I must say I've never experienced any desire to set foot in that country again. Our first stop was in Japan, I believe at Yakota Air Base. I bought a Miranda SLR camera at the PX during our short layover there.

We then flew all night toward home, and just as dawn was breaking, Mt. Rainier's peak came into view, protruding from the thick clouds and illuminated by the rising sun. What a beautiful and welcoming sight that was! We landed at SeaTac International Airport outside Seattle in a heavy fog and then loaded on buses for the trip to Fort Lewis, Washington (the final leg of my military career). It took all day to out-process from the Army, and I must have walked miles visiting all the clearing stations.

I finally got to call Janie later in the afternoon, and I really wish we had a recording of the conversation. I remember her first words were, "Where are you? Your voice is so clear!" When I responded that I was in Washington, she exploded into happy tears. Fortunately, she and Shannon had stayed in Houston after her parents had tried their best to get her to accompany them to Austin/Lakeway for the weekend. I would have been so lost if I had not been able to reach her on that call!

By the time I finished processing out of the Army, it was late, and there were no more flights headed toward Texas. My seat on the U.S.-bound plane had been in front of an exit and could not be reclined, and I had been unable to sleep on the flight. We had been up for a full day and night before we boarded, so I had not slept in at least sixty-five hours. I was exhausted but determined to get home, so I caught a cab back to SeaTac and began searching for flights going southeast. I think it took three flights on regional carriers, but I finally arrived at Houston International on Sunday, January 16, 1972, about 6:00 a.m. As I cleared the gate into the giant hallway, I spotted my beautiful girls headed toward me—the happiest day of my life! Janie asked Shannon if she knew who I was, and she said, "Da Da" and toddled right up to me.

The people walking past were no doubt oblivious to the young family in their joyous embrace, and this had probably happened a million times during the days of Vietnam. All major airports seemed packed with servicemen back then, but it struck me that most of us were essentially invisible to our fellow countrymen who couldn't imagine the life-changing experiences from which we were returning.

The Dallas Cowboys were playing the Miami Dolphins in the Super Bowl that Sunday, and I tried to stay awake to watch it, even though I'd had no sleep in seventy-six hours. I suffered from malaise and a cough for about a month after my return, which was probably related to the constant dampness, the all-night exposure to chilly sea breezes in Da Nang, and some serious jet lag.

Dear Janie

***

Registration at Stephen F. Austin State University began Wednesday, January 20, 1972. Janie and I raced to Lufkin, found a two-bedroom mobile home to rent, and got our utilities connected. As of that morning, I was a registered graduate student. It was a surreal transition from being a Soldier in a war zone 8,900 miles away to being a college student in Texas studying parasitology and biogenic amines within a week. I remember how difficult it was to focus on my studies which seemed to have no pertinence whatsoever to our new life. Dumping servicemen abruptly into civilian life, straight from war, seems archaic and even unappreciative, at best.

During that semester at SFA, I was hired by the Upjohn Company as a pharmaceutical sales representative—a job I loved. That probably came about largely due to my Army experience and especially my time at the 85th Evac.

Janie and I have been married now for 53 years and raised three beautiful daughters, Shannon Hofmann, Jessica Nester, and Cameron Bradley. They each married fine men and gave us seven terrific grandchildren. Certainly, the hard times made us better appreciate the good times and especially strengthened our love for each other. We are very much aware of how blessed our lives have been and give our sincere thanks to our Lord for the plan He so obviously had for us.

EPILOGUE

I graduated from Lufkin High School in Lufkin, Texas in 1964. Lufkin's population was approximately 16,000 at that time, and our senior class numbered 203 students. Our 50th reunion in 2014 was well attended, and I got to visit with old friends, many of whom I'd not seen since graduation. From various conversations, it became apparent that we had lost touch with one another largely because so many were drafted right out of high school and most were in Vietnam within two years unless they attended college. College allowed a four-year deferment from the draft, so some of us were inducted four years later. My classmates Bill Conrad, Mike Jones, and I then began trying to identify how many of us served during the Vietnam era. Ultimately, we came up with thirty-two out of our 109 male students. Not all of us went to Nam, primarily based on the luck of the draw. Some have suffered from Agent Orange and PTSD, but only one of our class was killed in action: Ted Jason Bishop.

Ted was a very outgoing guy and most everyone in our class considered him a friend. He, Fant Smart, and I were especially close growing up. We hunted, fished, water skied, shot archery, played ball, and did Scouting together. We also enjoyed cruising around town in Ted's brother's '31 Model A Roadster. Ted joined the Marines after attending Stephen F. Austin State University for about two years. He had attended a gunsmithing school after dropping out of SFA, and when the draft got closer, he told me the Marines promised he would be assigned to an ordnance depot since he had experience with gun repair. I wish I knew how he ended up in Force Reconnaissance, some of the "baddest of the bad" Marines. He was ultimately killed by gunfire in an ambush in Quảng Trị, the most northern province of Nam, along with two more members of their six-man recon team.

Almost all that I know of the events surrounding Ted's death came from a book written by Maj. Bruce H. "Doc" Norton, USMC (Ret.) titled *Force Recon Diary, 1969* (published by Ballantine Books in 1991). The author was a Navy Hospital Corpsman (HM3) at that time and had volunteered to serve with one of the six-man recon teams. The Marines have no trained medical personnel that are organic to their organization, so Navy Corpsmen are assigned to fill the role that medics serve in the Army. Almost all corpsmen and medics became known as "Doc" within their units. I highly recommend this book, especially to gain insight and a feel for the camaraderie, emotions, planning, training, and loyalty that go into tense combat operations. What we saw at the 85th Evac was only a snapshot of the results of combat. Seldom did we see the "rest of the story," which is so well captured by Maj. Norton. I have been fortunate to talk to Maj. Norton while writing this narrative.

In the next-to-last chapter titled, "Death in the A Shau Valley," Norton describes the helicopter extraction of the bodies of Sgt. Garcia, Lance Corporal Furhman, and Corporal Ted Bishop along with their surviving comrades from the A Shau Valley. PFC (private first class) Murray and Lance Corporal Silva survived the attack uninjured, but Lance Corporal Paul Keaveney suffered five gunshot wounds. He was the fourth man in a line of six. The first three were killed. Norton put me in touch with Keaveney. When I talked to him, I felt honored that he would share the details of that fateful mission. Keaveney was awarded the Silver Star for his actions during the ambush that took the life of our dear friend Ted Bishop. Following is a paragraph from Norton's book that reflects the shock of losing close friends and comrades that is undoubtedly typical of all wars.

> "When I walked into the squad bay, I was met by corporal Snowden, an assistant team leader in our platoon. He had already heard about the ambush, and he sat on the end of his rack, crying. I didn't have to speak to him, there was nothing that I could say. I wanted to know who was still alive and who had been killed. There were so many questions that remained unanswered. When would the team be extracted? Could whoever was still alive hold out until the Blue Team arrived? How could this have happened? When would we go over to the hospital and find out the answers to these questions?"

All six of the team members were brought to the 85th Evac. This happened February 7, 1970. I didn't arrive there until September 1971. Knowing the layout of the hospital I can see in my mind's eye the events described by Maj. Norton. I'm glad I was not a witness to them! Ironically, one of our Lufkin classmates Bill Conrad was a Force Recon Captain encamped at Hai Van Pass, just to the east of the A Shau. One of his Marines learned of the ongoing ambush and told Bill that one of those killed was from Lufkin and his initials were T. B. Names were never to be broadcast openly.

Another Third force Recon team had been ambushed two days earlier and three of its members were also killed. February 8, 1970, friends and fellow teammates were asked to deliver eulogies for their comrades. Doc Norton delivered Ted's, which was preserved in his book as follows:

> "Ted Bishop was the best team leader in our platoon. He cared about each one of us in his team, and he was always a friend to each one of us. Ted Bishop was a kind man, and he believed in God. He left us too soon. He has gone to a place that we know is a far better place than where we have been lately. We all will miss him, and we are better off and stronger for having known him. He taught us well, and for that we will always be thankful. Goodbye, Ted, and thanks."

Norton's eulogy was spot on for Ted, as he clearly exhibited remarkable leadership and courage as a Marine team leader. However, he had another side that not many were aware of. He wrote poetry. Somewhere I have a booklet of his poems, but the one that follows reflects his very soul. It was included in *Vietnam: "By Word of Mouth"* which was a Lufkin High School oral history project in 1988. Our daughter Shannon Slack Hofmann was one of the student contributors to the book.

Letters Home from 85th Evacuation Hospital Vietnam, 1971

Cpl. Ted Bishop and HM3 Bruce "Doc" Norton
1969 Vietnam

This War
By Ted Jason Bishop

I kill you not because of a dislike for you:
you are but one of a mass challenging my supremacy.
I see you not as the individual you surely must be,
for there is not time to think of this:
but rather, I must think of you as an object
without feeling or thoughts or loved ones.
Would you not strike me down
if I did not you first?
And yet, you know not of me.
What is it then that drives two strangers,
beings of the same race,
to take up arms against one another
and fight for the other's defeat?
It is because our people are at war that you die,
fighting for a cause which you will
never see fulfilled.
Yet, those who live on to enjoy the victory
—will they,
who do not know of you, call your name?
No, you are no longer an individual to these people
but merely one of thousands.
Your loved ones will remember, though.
To them you won the cause,
and then there were the other thousands.
Return to dust now, soldier,
for you have lost nothing.

Letters Home from 85th Evacuation Hospital Vietnam, 1971

It is on behalf of the Lufkin High School class of 1964 that this endeavor is dedicated to our forever-young classmate and friend, Ted Bishop.

Ted Jason Bishop
1946-1970
1964 Lufkin High School Senior picture

Glossary

A&D - admissions and dispositions

ADJUTANT - administrative assistant to the hospital Commanding Officer

AIT - advanced individual training (usually follows completion of basic training)

AK47 - standard communist 7.62mm automatic rifle

AOD - administrative officer of the day

ARVN - Army of the Republic of Vietnam

BC - battle casualty

BIEN HOA - major air base near Saigon, stationing Army, Air Force, Navy, and Marine units

C-130 HERCULES - a four-engine turboprop airplane used extensively for troop, medivac, and cargo transport

CCN - Command and Control North. A highly classified special operations unit involved with reconnaissance, covert action, and psychological warfare

CHINOOK - CH-47 transport helicopter

CHOPPER - nickname given to helicopters

CO - Commanding Officer

COBRA - AH-1G helicopter gunship

DEROS - date eligible for return from overseas

DMZ - demilitarized zone (the boundary between North and South Vietnam)

DOA - dead on arrival

DUSTOFF - the emergency evacuation of casualties from a combat zone. Also, the callsign specific to U.S. Army medivac helicopters

ETS - expiration term of service (end of active-duty obligation)

FRAGGING - tossing a fragmentation grenade into sleeping area to murder an officer or NCO

FLAK JACKET - steel plated vest designed to deflect projectiles

GRAVES REGISTRATION - personnel responsible for recovering, reclaiming, processing, and returning the bodies to families for proper funerals and burials

GSW - gunshot wound

HI/BYE - usually a gathering for welcoming new personnel and wishing farewell to those leaving

HUEY - UH-1 helicopter. The predominate utility helicopter used in Vietnam

KIA - killed in action

LAW - light antitank weapon

LOH - light observation helicopter, also called Loach

LONG BIHN - site of the largest U.S. Army base in Vietnam. Situated between Bien Hoa airbase and Saigon, it was populated by 60,000 people

LTC - lieutenant colonel

LZ - landing zone

M14 - U.S. 7.62 mm selective-fire rifle

M16 - standard issue U.S. 5.56 mm automatic rifle

M79 - standard U.S. 40 mm grenade launcher

MACV - U.S. Military Assistance Command, Vietnam. A joint service command of the United States Department of Defense based at Tan Son Nhut Air Base near Siagon

MAMASAN - the name given to female civilian workers. A polite title, coined by US soldiers in Japan after WWII

Letters Home from 85th Evacuation Hospital Vietnam, 1971

MIA - missing in action

MOS - Military Occupational Specialty

NCO - noncommissioned officer (pay grades E4 to E9)

NEWBIES - new personnel to Nam (more commonly known as FNG's or f---ing new guys)

NVA - North Vietnamese Army

OCS - Officer Candidate School

OJT - on the job training

PSC - perforated or pierced steel planking

REMF - rear-echelon motherf....r

ROTC - Reserve Officer Training Corps

RPG - rocket-propelled grenade

R&R - rest and recreation leave

S2 - intelligence officer at battalion or brigade level

2/17 - Second of the Seventeenth: 2nd Squadron, 17th Calvary Regiment, 101st Airborne Division

SHORT - short time remaining to be served in Nam (Deros)

SLICK - UH-1 Huey used primarily for transport (not a dustoff or gunship)

TRIAGE - assessment of casualties to determine the urgency of their need and the nature of treatment required

USARV - U.S. Army Vietnam

VC - Viet Cong; communist guerrilla movement that fought the U.S. and South Vietnamese government forces with the support of the North Vietnamese Army, commonly referred to as "Charlie" by GI's

WIA - wounded in action

WP - white phosphorus, also called "Willie Pete"

XO - executive officer

ABOUT THE AUTHOR

James Slack grew up in Lufkin, Texas. He earned a BA in Vertebrate Zoology from the University of Texas at Austin in 1968 and taught high school Chemistry and Biology in Crockett, Texas before being commissioned as a Second Lieutenant in the U.S. Army Medical Service Corps in 1969. James served two years at Ft. Gordon, Georgia before being assigned as Registrar for the 85th Evacuation Hospital in Phu Bai, Vietnam in 1971. Upon completing his military commitment, he worked eight years in the pharmaceutical industry with the Upjohn Company in Marshall and Dallas, Texas. Following a career change, he retired in 2012 after serving thirty years as a banker in his hometown.

James is active in various civic activities and has served on numerous committees and boards, including the Rotary Club, Planning and Zoning Commission, Woodland Heights Medical Center, Blood Center East Texas, and the Gulf Coast Regional Blood Center in Houston. He is a multi-gallon blood donor. Slack is recipient of two of his community's highest awards for community service.

James has served as a deacon and then an elder for over thirty years with his church in Lufkin. Bass fishing and bow hunting are his favorite outdoor activities.

He and his beloved wife, Janie, have been married for over 53 years and raised three daughters Shannon, Jessica, and Cameron. Now, they have been blessed with three sons-in-law John, Lee, and Deacon plus seven grandchildren!

Made in United States
Orlando, FL
09 June 2024